Round the Circle

Related Publications

Educating Young Children: Active Learning Practices in Preschool and Child Care Programs

Movement in Steady Beat

Movement Plus Music: Activities for Children Ages 3 to 7, Second Edition

Movement Plus Rhymes, Songs, & Singing Games, Second Edition

Movement Plus Rhymes, Songs, & Singing Games (cassette, CD)

Rhythmically Moving 1–9 (cassettes, CDs)

Guides to Rhythmically Moving 1–4

Teaching Movement & Dance: A Sequential Approach to Rhythmic Movement, Fourth Edition

Other Movement and Dance Publications

Beginning Folk Dances Illustrated 1–5 (videos)

Changing Directions 1–6 (cassettes, CDs)

Cultures and Styling in Folk Dance

Foundations in Elementary Education: Movement

Foundations in Elementary Education: Music

Foundations in Elementary Education: Music Recordings (cassette, CD)

Teaching Folk Dance: Successful Steps

Teaching Folk Dance 1 & 2 (teaching videotapes)

Available from

High/Scope® Press

600 North River Street
Ypsilanti, Michigan 48198-2898

ORDERS: phone (800) 40-PRESS, fax (800) 442-4FAX

Web site: www.highscope.org

Round the Circle

Key Experiences in Movement for Young Children

Second edition, completely revised and expanded

Phyllis S. Weikart

HIGH/SCOPE® PRESS

Ypsilanti, Michigan

Published by

HIGH/SCOPE® PRESS

A division of the

High/Scope® Educational Research Foundation
600 North River Street
Ypsilanti, Michigan 48198-2898
(734) 485-2000, FAX (734) 485-0704

High/Scope Press Editor: Lynn Taylor

Cover design, text design, and production: Judy Seling of Seling Design

Library of Congress Cataloging-in-Publication Data

Weikart, Phyllis S., 1931-
    Round the circle : key experiences in movement for young children / Phyllis S.
Weikart.–2nd ed., completely rev. and expanded.
        p. cm.
    Includes bibliographical references and index.
    ISBN 1-57379-096-6
    1. Movement education. 2. Physical education for children. I. Title.

GV452 .W438 2000
372.86'044--dc21   00-56704

Printed in the United States of America

10 9 8 7 6 5 4 3

Contents

3 Enabling the Learner: Ways to Move 61

Acknowledgments

I wish to thank all the individuals who have helped me bring increased depth of understanding to the motor development and overall development of the preschool-aged child since this book was first published in 1986. These individuals include my friend Connie Wright, a physical education colleague from Gwinnett, Georgia, who has been working with kindergarten children and discovering that their motor development is lagging way behind chronological age. I also thank my friend Libby Carlton from Salisbury, North Carolina, the developer of the High/Scope music key experiences, who has presented early childhood movement and music workshops and 4-week training programs with me throughout the United States. We have learned so much from the participants in these training events and from our discussions and planning for the sessions. In addition, Libby's grandchildren and my grandchildren have served as an "ongoing lab" for us in the development of the young child from birth to age 5. To Libby and to Connie, I express my deep gratitude for all they have done to assist me over the years. Both are adjunct trainers in the High/Scope *Education Through Movement: Building the Foundation* program and have served as lead assistants in the High/Scope summer movement and music training sessions.

Other adjunct trainers in the movement program who have provided additional ideas and support over the years we have worked together are as follows: Beverly Boardman from Sarasota, Florida; Beth Bryant from Barre, Massachusetts; Kristin Goodnight from Melbourne, Florida; Liz Haraksin from Riverside, California; Janet Hutson-Brandhagen from Lynnwood, Washington; Penny Mahoney from Hadley, Massachusetts; and Karen Sawyers from Springfield, Tennessee. I also wish to thank Chris Ashley, Assistant Director of the High/Scope *Education Through Movement: Building the Foundation* program, for working with draft copies of two of the chapters of this book.

To my family I express heartfelt appreciation for their loyal support. My husband, David, and daughters, Cindy, Cathy, Jenny, and Gretchen, are always there for me and provide much-appreciated support.

Finally, I wish to thank my editor, Lynn Taylor, for her keen observations. My thanks are also extended to Pattie McDonald, who prepared the manuscript for publication, and to Judy Seling of Seling Design for the special graphic design and layout of this book.

Introduction

This book has been written primarily for those adults who work with and care for children before they reach kindergarten: preschool teachers, music and physical education specialists, child care providers, and parents. Because the audience is so varied, technical jargon has been used only when absolutely necessary.

The activities described are most appropriate for 3- to 5-year-olds, although there is a brief review of activities for infants and toddlers in Chapter 1. Also, adults working with children in the early elementary grades should find the suggested activities useful for their students.[1]

Over the many years I have worked with children and adults in movement activities and in organized folk dance, I have observed that many of them could not perform simple motor patterns. For example, many could not walk to the beat of the music; many could not do a simple movement in unison with others. When questioned about a movement just performed, both children and adults seemed to lack the awareness of how their bodies had moved. In addition, many of the younger children I worked with lacked the ability to talk about movements they had performed or to plan movements they could perform. Moreover, both younger and older children had difficulty imitating simple patterns and following simple verbal directions for movement.

We recognize that young children learn through their movements and play—through being *active.* Thus the development of movement (gross-motor) skills in young children results from their direct experiences, and adults need to encourage and support children appropriately as they engage in these naturally

Young children learn through their movements and play . . . through being active. Motor skills are the direct result of experience and practice with the appropriate support of observant adults.

---

[1]Adults who work with older students will find helpful information in *Teaching Movement & Dance: A Sequential Approach to Rhythmic Movement* (Weikart, 1998), and *Teaching Folk Dance: Successful Steps* (Weikart, 1997). Also of interest to adults working with elementary-aged children, teens, and adults is *Cultures and Styling in Folk Dance* (Longden & Weikart, 1998), which covers the history, choreographic origins, instruments and music, and traditional clothing and costumes of the dances. In addition, nine *Rhythmically Moving* and six *Changing Directions* recordings have been produced to accompany my books. Throughout this book, reference is made to these titles, especially the recordings, to highlight the interconnectedness of the movement and music materials I have produced.

occurring learning activities in infancy and early childhood. When adults understand the significance of early gross-motor development, of "natural play," and of talking with children about *their* interests and experiences, they can support children by *labeling their actions* and *by asking them questions to stimulate their thinking.* Without early opportunities to engage in such active learning situations, many young children begin kindergarten with inadequate motor skill development, and they do not acquire these gross-motor skills through "natural" experiences later on in life. In fact, it appears that today's children have fewer opportunities than did children in previous generations for constructive movement, play, and language interaction with adults and peers. Why? In my view, there seem to be several possible reasons:

- **First and foremost among the reasons is the excessive amount of time many children devote to viewing television and videos and playing computer games.** A cautionary word is provided here about the detrimental effects of children's excessive television viewing on their overall development. According to author Carla Hannaford (1995, p. 171), "The average American child watches 3 hours of TV a day with one-fourth [of the children] watching more than 6 hours of TV a day." She also quotes the A. C. Nielsen Company's *Nielsen Report on Television 1990,* "American preschool children ages 2–5 years watch television over 27 hours per week." (Hannaford, 1995, p. 171). In her book *Endangered Minds, Why Children Don't Think and What We Can Do About It* (1990), Jane Healy recommends that television be banned for children before the age of 8 so that their imagination and language skills will have a chance to be established. Eric Jensen (1998, p. 22) seems to agree with Healy: "Television provides no time for reflection, interactions, or 3-dimensional visual development. TV is 2-dimensional, and the developing brain needs depth. TV moves fast and talks about abstractions that are often nonexistent in the child's development. The eyes have no time to relax." Robert Siege and William Dietz, quoted in an article by Raymond Kessler in the *Journal of Pediatrics* (October 1994), state that American children spend more time watching television than attending school. This information follows an earlier report by Carol Tomlinson-Keasey (1985, p. 26) that television viewing actually consumes more time in a child's life than any other activity except sleeping.

  The waking hours children spend in front of a television, if excessive, rob them of the time needed for valuable *adult-child interactions* and for *play experiences.* During the formative years, these interactions and experiences directly affect the development of a child's brain and the degree to which that child will function to his or her full potential. In addition, these passive activities may make it more difficult for children to pay attention and to concentrate in the classroom and home because of the shorter attention spans that result from the quickly changing scenes and events portrayed on television and videos. Also, such passivity may cause children to be less fit physically which, in turn, could increase the risk of future heart disease.

- **Today's trend toward smaller families means that children may have fewer siblings and fewer neighborhood friends to play with informally,** and this can adversely affect a child's gross-motor development. Young children who do not have siblings and neighborhood children to play with may miss many enjoyable opportunities to engage informally and spontaneously in physical games and activities and to imitate their other siblings' actions and movements.

- **Neighborhood play areas are often scarce, and where they do exist, they are difficult for adults to supervise.** In many cities and large urban areas, often there are not enough nearby areas where children can run about and play freely and safely without adults present. Children thus are not able to experience the joy and freedom of spontaneous play activities and naturally occurring physical challenges.

While playing with her children at preschool, this mother encourages her younger child to imitate his older brother's movements. Mom is also supporting the children's crawling action by crawling along with them!

- **Increasing numbers of children are being placed in child care and preschool programs by their parents.** In child care as well as in preschool, there often is not enough space or adult support for the kind of play that encourages gross-motor skill development. Also, in today's drive for academic learning to occur at younger and younger ages, caregivers may not realize the educational significance of informal play to a young child's motor development and overall physical and mental development.

- **Finally, from my experience, it appears that many adults who work with young children do not know what children of a given age can and should be doing in movement.** Many caregivers and even some teachers seem to lack guidelines and concrete ideas for facilitating the motor development of young children. Please refer to the "Expectations for Children by Kindergarten," page 13, in this chapter for guidelines in this area.

For all of these reasons, and to help solve the related problems, I have developed **eight key experiences in movement** for young children, and these are the focus of this book. These movement key experiences are the result of numerous workshop and conference presentations, experience working with many populations of children on movement awareness activities, and the things I have learned as I play with my own grandchildren. I have found that the eight key experiences have two major benefits:

- They help 3- to 5-year-old children develop and strengthen their motor coordination abilities.

- They prepare children to be successful in future movement, music, and classroom experiences.

Before considering these key experiences, however, we should review the reasons why motor coordination in young children is so important to their overall development.

The Importance of Successful Early Movement Experiences

Early movement experiences have the potential to greatly enhance a child's self-concept because movement experiences are so personal and because success depends so much on one's own skills and abilities. It is essential that parents, teachers, and caregivers provide positive reinforcement—and lots of it—when young children attempt movement activities. Adults should recognize and acknowledge young children's explorations and experimentation and encourage them to continue to work on developing their movement skills.

When such a positive atmosphere for movement exploration is established and maintained, young children may be more willing to try new things in other areas as well. These new opportunities for successful learning may increase children's confidence in their intellectual as well as physical abilities. Unsuccessful movement experiences, however, can erode a child's self-concept. Suppose someone tells a child that he or she didn't do it "right" before the child has had enough time and opportunity to master a specific skill. This premature negative feedback can destroy the child's incentive for more practice. No one wants to fail!

Consider a child who is trying to learn to kick a ball. If no one is around, that child may experiment with many ways of using the foot to move the ball. The child will keep trying even when unsuccessful in completing the task of moving the ball, because more and more success is occurring with each try. The following scenario illustrates what happens when adults do not realize the importance of supporting young children at their level of physical, mental, and social development.

John and his young son, Brian, are at the beach. John decides it is time to introduce Brian to the wonders of baseball by showing him how to use a bat to hit the baseball. He positions his son in the "correct" batting posture and moves away to pitch the ball. Brian turns to face his dad, with the bat on his shoulder, waiting for the pitch. John throws up his hands and walks back to Brian to re-position him in the "correct" batting posture. This sequence occurs two more times. At this point, Brian throws down the bat and goes off to play in a pile of sand.

Lauren is happily learning to kick a ball. Because she has lots of room to experiment, she is free to try many ways of kicking the ball.

If an adult, as in the above example, criticizes a child's initial attempts at mastering a movement, or expects a child to master the movement in an adult way, the child's desire to explore and experiment, which is needed for ultimate success in movement activities, may be quickly squelched. Realizing the risk of failure, a child like Brian simply stops trying. If, however, a supportive adult is present when a young child is engaging in early movement experiences, and the adult participates with the child *at the child's level* and encourages the child to continue, then both the child and the adult will have a positive and successful experience.

Allison, age 3½, is only hopping on her preferred side, thus creating a half-skip movement. Her grandmother watches her and says, "Oh, Allison, you're hopping on one foot!" (Grandma has acknowledged the child's movement in a supportive way and has labeled it for the child.) Grandma then points to Allison's other leg and suggests, "Now maybe you could use your other foot as you hop, Allison!" Later that day, after supporting Allison through several attempts to gallop with the other foot leading, Grandma watches as Allison begins to gallup successfully. Then Allison tries to skip again, and Grandma once more offers encouragement and support as she spends a few minutes chanting "BA, ba, BA, ba" to Allison's uneven skip rhythm. Occasionally, Allison reverts back to the half-skip, and Grandma offers encouragement for this effort as well. A week later, again playing with Grandma, Allison uses her new motor skills with a great deal of confidence, and she skips along without reverting back to the half-skip of the week before.

Clearly, the foundation for successful movement experiences begins to take shape when the child is very young and continues to form throughout that child's lifetime. At any stage of this process, if the child's teacher (whether parent, caregiver, or educator) lacks sufficient knowledge of motor development, what may actually be a young child's successful initial attempt at mastering a movement can be turned into a resounding failure. We all have heard people tell stories of early experiences that were damaging to them—a friend who was picked last for games because of poor skills; another who was told not to sing in the concert so as not to spoil the sound; another who was made to feel foolish and clumsy in front of peers in dance class.

This book is written to help adults learn how to help children avoid such negative experiences and instead help them engage in successful early movement experiences that foster positive self-concepts. My hope is that (1) a broad audience of early childhood educators, caregivers, and parents will be reached through this book; (2) more young children will experience success with gross-motor skills and movement patterns because their teachers will have a clearer idea of how to initiate movement activities in a simple and appropriate manner; and (3) children will gain more positive self-concepts in relation to their movement abilities, which will in turn help them be more successful in their overall school performance. In particular, I want us to reach, albeit in an indirect way, the many children who seem to feel they are failures before they even enter school. As noted earlier, this perception of failure may be created by well-intentioned adults who try to "teach" these children important concepts and skills and, in the teaching process, find it necessary to judge the child's performance negatively instead of encouraging the child to keep trying. Who among us wants to be told over and over that we are failing? How long before this sense of failure would cause *us* to stop trying?

As noted at the beginning of this chapter, this book focuses on the 3-, 4-, and 5-year-old child, but information is also included on supporting children's movement experiences before the age of 3.[2] To set the stage for the key experiences in movement for 3- to 5-year-olds, let us first consider movement experiences that are appropriate for infants and toddlers.

Movement Experiences for Infants and Toddlers

Infants explore their world through their senses and through their movements. They learn about their environment as they see, hear, reach, grasp, roll over, sit, squirm, and crawl on hands and knees. As toddlers, young children explore their world in more expansive ways. They learn to manipulate objects, to understand

---

[2]Persons working with children in the early elementary grades will also find this book useful, because many elementary-aged children will not have had the early movement experiences described in the following chapters. In addition, two other books, *Foundations in Elementary Education: Movement* (Weikart & Carlton, 1995) and *Foundations in Elementary Education: Music* (Carlton & Weikart, 1994), will be useful to adults working with elementary-aged children.

language, and to describe what they are doing. With regard to motor skill development, they become more aware of their bodies and what their bodies can do. They learn that they can move their bodies purposefully to do many things. They learn these skills through *direct experience*.

Consider as an example of this developmental level 2-year-old Maria who is playing near her mom. Mom is preparing a cake, in the kitchen. Maria watches her mom and then decides to pull pots, pans, and other cooking utensils out of a kitchen drawer that she can reach. Her mom watches carefully, but doesn't stop the activity. Then, using stirring motions to imitate her mother's motions, Maria pretends to make a cake just like her mom is doing. Her mom "plays along" and

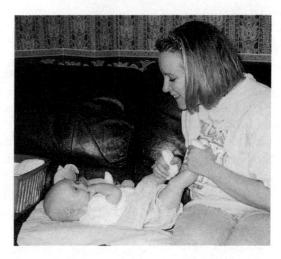

It's easy to help an infant feel the underlying beat of a musical selection, song, or rhyme. Infants, like Caitlin, hear and respond to sounds, to voices, and to music. Caitlin has just had a diaper change, and her mom, Christy, is pumping Caitlin's legs to the underlying steady beat of the song she is singing to her.

pretends with Maria. After a while, Maria begins to put the pans together and then takes them apart. Finally, Maria places the items back in the drawer but then decides to remove them once again!

Adults and older children are pivotal in supporting motor skill development in young children like Maria. Like Maria's mom, we can encourage a child to explore further and can provide positive reinforcement for the child's successes. Sometimes, however, we may discourage children's movement opportunities and activities because we fear for their safety or do not wish to see our house or center in disarray. While a child's personal safety should always be considered, we should also understand that young children need many naturally occurring opportunities to master their early motor skills.

Why the push to make sure children are active both physically and mentally? Carla Hannaford, quoted in the *Teaching Elementary Physical Education* newsletter (November 1998, p. 18), states, "Movement activates the neural wiring through the body, making the whole body the instrument of learning. Beginning in infancy and continuing through our lives, physical movement plays an essential role in creating nerve cell networks that are the essence of learning." Writing in a different issue of the newsletter (December 1996, p. 6), Rae Pica focuses on the importance of movement in the preschool years: "The preschool years are an exciting time for motor development. Three-year-olds begin to move with greater ease and grace, and by the time they are five, preschoolers are executing most, if not all, the basic locomotor and nonlocomotor skills." Based on my own experience, I believe that preschoolers will learn these basic skills if they have many opportunities for natural and spontaneous physical play. Today's experts in child development seem to agree that children in preschool and elementary school should spend at least an hour each day in physical activity.

It is clear that parents and caregivers, in particular, can encourage children's motor skill development from a very early age. In the infant's first month of life, for example, parents can begin to foster one of the most important early foundations for later motor skill development: the infant's **awareness of the steady beat.** This awareness is the foundation on which the child builds future motor coordination. An inability to feel steady beat often creates problems for children in many different learning situations.

It's quite easy to help the infant feel the underlying beat of a musical selection, song, or rhyme. The newborn's hearing is fully developed at birth, so the infant can hear and respond to sounds, voices, and music. The adult just has to pat or stroke the infant to the underlying **steady beat** while chanting or singing to the child, or while playing music on the radio or stereo. Such "hands-on guidance," or tactile stimulation, helps the infant become aware of the *feel* of steady beat. Consider, for example, such a common infant/adult activity as rocking. Holding a child and rocking usually is performed to a slow, strongly accented beat, which the infant can easily feel. The rocking action not only is very soothing but also involves total body movement, as does holding an infant while singing or chanting or dancing to music. The infant can hear the chant or the song or the recorded music *and* can feel the steady beat generated in these chants, songs, and recorded musical selections.

In these circumstances, it is important that adults be able to understand the difference between **moving to the steady beat** and *moving to the rhythm of the words.* An infant will not necessarily learn to feel the underlying steady beat of a song or rhyme if the caregiver holding her is moving to the rhythm of the words. To illustrate this point, let's consider the simple rhyme "Patty cake, patty cake, baker's man." If the syllables of words are emphasized, there will be three movements for each verbalized "patty cake," two movements for the two syllables of "baker's," and one movement for "man." If the *steady beat of the rhyme* is emphasized, however, there will be **four movements of equal duration.** Here's a graphic illustration of this essential difference:

	Pat-ty	Cake	Pat-ty	Cake	Bak-er's	Man
Rhythm of words	x x	x	x x	x	x x	x
Steady beat of rhyme	x		x		x	x

The child should be able to feel steady beat and walk to that steady beat by age 3. This **steady beat competence** forms the movement foundation that permits a child to acquire the basic motor skills of early childhood without difficulty.

Many other motor skills are emerging at the infant and toddler stages. Infants and toddlers need lots of space so that they can wiggle their arms and legs freely, learn to roll over, sit up, pull up to a standing position, and eventually walk. They need objects to touch, feel, and throw. In short, they need appropriate physical as well as mental challenges that encourage them to actively explore their environment and the objects in it.

Simple movement experiences can greatly enhance the young child's developing motor skills. Consider creeping or crawling, for example. Youngsters who learn to stand and walk at an early age may not have crawled enough to master opposite arm and leg coordination. Learning to coordinate the opposite arm and leg required to produce the fluid motion of crawling seems to be an integral link to later weight-bearing movements that require similar coordination of the opposite arm and leg, such as throwing a ball, swimming, or dancing. Because crawling is so important, parents, caregivers, and teachers should encourage crawling activities, perhaps by crawling with the infant or toddler and making a game out of it.

Youngsters also need to experience many climbing activities. Climbing up and down stairs helps the youngster learn to transfer weight smoothly while leading first with one foot and then with the other. This skill helps children learn to use their nonpreferred side, an important ability they will need later when they want to learn more complex movements, such as skipping. Children should have ample opportunity to climb stairs, either at home or in other settings.

Youngsters also need many opportunities to imitate the movements of others. For example, an adult playing with an infant can squeeze her eyes shut, or shake her head, or wave her arms to see if the baby will imitate one of these motions. While playing with a toddler, an adult can put both arms in the air and ask the toddler to do the same, or the adult can bend low to the ground and wait for the child to imitate the movement. Whichever movement is explored, the adult should maintain the position long enough to give the child ample time to copy it; also, the movement should be both simple and expansive. Toddlers will enjoy taking the initiative in these spontaneous games and should be encouraged to do so.

An infant's or toddler's motor skill development also can be greatly enhanced by simple language activities such as asking them to follow or imitate simple verbal directions. For example, the adult could imitate an infant's sounds and then encourage

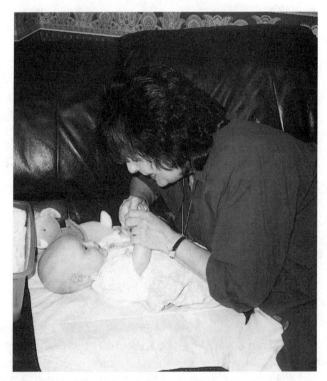

Four-month-old Caitlin is playing "Patty Cake" with her grandma. She's just beginning to understand that Grandma's words are connected to the hand movements they are doing together. Caitlin doesn't understand the concept of steady beat yet, but her grandma is also helping her experience the steady beat of the rhyme with the patting motion.

These young children are using opportunities to experiment with climbing. Through experience, children gradually learn to alternate their feet as they climb.

him to make the sound again. With a toddler, the adult could ask her, "Show me where your ball is. Please bring me the ball." At the beginning of these types of interactions it may be helpful to provide visual cues, such as pointing, *after* giving the oral instructions. But later on, when the child is accustomed to responding to the verbal directions, the visual cues should not be needed.

Engaging or being engaged in meaningful conversation is another important aspect of a young child's overall development and also plays a major role in motor skill development. With an infant, adults can make it a habit to describe what is occurring: "Now I am going to turn you over and change your diaper." "Now we are going to sit down and put on your snowsuit." "Now it is time to sit at the table and eat your lunch." With toddlers, adults can pose questions to encourage the child to talk about what he or she is doing: "What are you going to do with that ball, Latisha?" "Eddie, what are you building with your blocks?" "Christy, what are you pretending to be when you move like that?" In responding to such questions and statements, young children gradually begin to realize that different parts of the body can do different things and can move in different ways. Children also begin to realize that their thoughts and ideas are important to adults.

Another important language experience—reading—can also foster motor skill competence in both infants and toddlers. By pretending to move like the characters or animals described in a story the adult is reading to the child, adults can gradually introduce relevant movements.

These are just a few of the enjoyable and natural occurring experiences in which adults and young children can engage to enhance the infant's and toddler's motor skill development.

Movement Experiences for Preschoolers

Such experiences as just described for infants and toddlers form the foundation for the **eight key experiences in movement** for 3- to 5-year-olds that are the focus of this book:

- *Acting upon movement directions*

- *Describing movement*

- *Moving in nonlocomotor ways*

- *Moving in locomotor ways*

- *Moving with objects*

- *Expressing creativity in movement*

- *Feeling and expressing steady beat*

- *Moving in sequences to a common beat*

The key experiences in movement provide a range of important basic movement activities. These key experiences form the foundation for children's later success in physical education and music curricula and can also have a positive impact on children's overall school performance. The movement key experiences help young children succeed in school because they meet the following educational needs:

- Provide basic movement coordination experiences for the young child who is learning through active, physical exploration.

- Develop the child's body awareness and space awareness

- Extend the child's attention span by providing learning opportunities that strengthen aural comprehension and visual perception skills

- Create an awareness in the child of steady beat as the child learns to move to the beat.

- Help the child develop a positive self-concept.

These eight key experiences are presented in Chapters 2–4 and are organized under three major headings: **"engaging the learner," "enabling the learner,"** and **"extending the learner."** Each discussion provides a general description of the particular key experience, describes the methods recommended for introducing the experience to preschoolers, and offers suggested activities. *These eight key experiences should be viewed as the basic building blocks that are necessary to support a child's overall gross-motor development.*

Expectations for Children by Kindergarten

What should be the movement expectations for children by the time they reach kindergarten? The following is a list of gross-motor abilities and skills that are attainable by kindergarten. These skills are most easily mastered while the child is young, but the experiential nature of them allows them to be explored and mastered at any age:

Work time in the preschool is a good time to encourage children to travel on a block roadway they have constructed.

- Creeping and crawling

- Starting and stopping without falling down

- Climbing up and down stairs with a change of lead foot

- Rolling and tumbling

- Throwing, kicking, catching, striking balls

- Identifying parts of the body and knowing how they move

- Moving about without bumping into others

- Imitating simple sequences of movements

- Responding to simple sequences of verbal directions

- Talking about what one is doing, planning what to do, and recalling correctly how one moved

- Synchronizing a single motion with a single word (learner SAY & DO)

- Walking to a musical beat

- Walking, running, jumping, hopping, galloping, sliding, skipping, with relative ease of movement

I have prepared a "Movement Observation Record" instrument (presented on page 15) that you can use to assess the movement development of preschoolers. Once you are familiar with the contents of this book, you will find this instrument to be useful in keeping track of individual children's motor development.

When to Introduce the Key Experiences in Movement

Movement activities for preschoolers are good icebreakers, transition-time activities, and attention-getters. For example, in a preschool or child care setting use them to begin a segment of the day—planning time, work time, snack time, review time—or to start a lengthier block of time for working with the other High/Scope key experiences (see list on page 16.) Movement activities can also be used to enhance large-group time or outdoor time; to provide a short greeting or good-bye time at the beginning or end of the day; or just to add some purposeful movement to the daily routine.[3]

The main things to remember about introducing the key experiences in movement to young children are these:

1. **Keep them short.**

2. **Keep them simple.**

3. **Make them enjoyable.**

4. **Design them to assure success.**

5. **Follow the children's interests.**

Turn now to Chapter 1 to learn about the movement-based active learning process in terms of the eight key experiences, an essential **movement core,** a **teaching model,** and strategies for promoting active learning. Chapters 2 through 4 examine the key experiences in detail, including specific suggestions for supporting children in these key learning areas. Chapter 5 presents important summary information for adults. General guidelines and reminders to adults for each of the eight key experiences are contained in this final chapter.

---

[3]For a complete description of the High/Scope preschool approach, see *Educating Young Children: Active Learning Practices for Preschool and Child Care Programs* (Hohmann & Weikart, 1995).

Movement Observation Record

The Movement Observation Record has 5 items of increasing difficulty under each heading. If the child is judged to be able to do item 3 in the list, items 1 and 2 should also be judged successful.

A. Moving in nonlocomotor and locomotor ways (exhibiting body coordination)
1. Child's movements appear awkward.
2. Child marches or runs smoothly.
3. Child gallops and jumps up and down.
4. Child walks up the stairs, alternating feet to the next stair.
5. Child engages in complex movements (hopping, skipping).

B. Moving with objects in purposeful ways
1. Child uses appropriate finger and hand motions to grasp and use objects.
2. Child moves about with scarves and ribbons.
3. Child uses objects such as beanbags and balls for throwing and kicking.
4. Child uses smaller objects, e.g., scissors, rhythm sticks, or unpitched percussion instruments.
5. Child engages in more complex movement with objects (dribbling a ball, batting or catching a tossed ball).

C. Responding to movement directions presented visually
1. Child has difficulty imitating a visual movement demonstration.
2. Child imitates single movement demonstrations.
3. Child imitates movement sequences of two different motions.
4. Child performs movement sequences presented visually using two to four body parts in the sequence.
5. Child copies a movement sequence for an action song presented visually.

D. Responding to verbal or sung movement directions
1. Child has difficulty attending to verbal or sung directions for movement.
2. Child follows verbal or sung directions for single movements.
3. Child follows verbal or sung directions for two-part movements ("Put your hands on your head and then on your shoulders").
4. Child follows verbal or sung directions for more complex sequences of movements ("Put your hands on top of your head; now put one hand on your ear and the other on your nose").
5. Child follows verbal or sung directions for an action song, then repeats the movement.

E. Feeling and expressing steady beat
1. Child does not yet imitate steady beat movements.
2. Child copies single movements performed to a steady beat (pats knees with hands).
3. Child copies single steady beat movements while listening to rhymes, songs, or instrumental music.
4. Child initiates single movements to the steady beat while listening to rhymes, songs, or instrumental music (patting knees, stepping the beat).
5. Child chants or sings while performing single steady beat movements.

F. Moving in sequences to a common beat
1. Child does not yet move in a sequence of two motions.
2. Child responds to a sequence of two motions performed slowly.
3. Child initiates a sequence of two different motions.
4. Child demonstrates a sequence of two different motions while verbally labeling the motions.
5. Child demonstrates a sequence of four different motions while verbally labeling the motions.

High/Scope Preschool Key Experiences

Creative Representation
- Recognizing objects by sight, sound, touch, taste, and smell
- Imitating actions and sounds
- Relating models, pictures, and photographs to real places and things
- Pretending and role playing
- Making models out of clay, blocks, and other materials
- Drawing and painting

Language and Literacy
- Talking with others about personally meaningful experiences
- Describing objects, events, and relations
- Having fun with language: listening to stories and poems, making up stories and rhymes
- Writing in various ways: drawing, scribbling, letterlike forms, invented spelling, conventional forms
- Reading in various ways: reading storybooks, signs and symbols, one's own writing
- Dictating stories

Initiative and Social Relations
- Making and expressing choices, plans, and decisions
- Solving problems encountered in play
- Taking care of one's own needs
- Expressing feelings in words
- Participating in group routines
- Being sensitive to the feelings, interests, and needs of others
- Building relationships with children and adults
- Creating and experiencing collaborative play
- Dealing with social conflict

Movement
- Moving in nonlocomotor ways (anchored movement: bending, twisting, rocking, swinging one's arms)
- Moving in locomotor ways (nonanchored movement: running, jumping, hopping, skipping, marching, climbing)
- Moving with objects
- Expressing creativity in movement
- Describing movement
- Acting upon movement directions
- Feeling and expressing steady beat
- Moving in sequences to a common beat

Music
- Moving to music
- Exploring and identifying sounds
- Exploring the singing voice
- Developing melody
- Singing songs
- Playing simple musical instruments

Classification
- Exploring and describing similarities, differences, and the attributes of things
- Distinguishing and describing shapes
- Sorting and matching
- Using and describing something in several ways
- Holding more than one attribute in mind at a time
- Distinguishing between "some" and "all"
- Describing characteristics something does not possess or what class it does not belong to

Seriation
- Comparing attributes (longer/shorter, bigger/smaller)
- Arranging several things one after another in a series or pattern and describing the relationships (big/bigger/biggest, red/blue/red/blue)
- Fitting one ordered set of objects to another through trial and error (small cup-small saucer/medium cup-medium saucer/big cup-big saucer)

Number
- Comparing the numbers of things in two sets to determine "more," "fewer," "same number"
- Arranging two sets of objects in one-to-one correspondence
- Counting objects

Space
- Filling and emptying
- Fitting things together and taking them apart
- Changing the shape and arrangement of objects (wrapping, twisting, stretching, stacking, enclosing)
- Observing people, places, and things from different spatial viewpoints
- Experiencing and describing positions, directions, and distances in the play space, building, and neighborhood
- Interpreting spatial relations in drawings, pictures, and photographs

Time
- Starting and stopping an action on signal
- Experiencing and describing rates of movement
- Experiencing and comparing time intervals
- Anticipating, remembering, and describing sequences of events

A Movement-Based Active Learning Process

The movement-based active learning process consists of four components:

- Eight key experiences in movement

- A movement core

- A teaching model

- Active learning strategies for movement

The Key Experiences in Movement

The **eight key experiences in movement** for children aged 3–5 provide the framework for the movement-based active learning process described here. We use these key experiences to recognize, support, and extend the preschooler's fundamental abilities in movement. These important key experiences affect many aspects of children's social, emotional, intellectual, and physical development.

Each movement key experience is developmentally sequenced and is described in terms of actions performed by young children. As noted in the Introduction, they are organized into three categories—**engaging the learner, enabling the learner,** and **extending the learner** (see Chart 1.1).

Taken together, these eight key experiences for young children are designed to build a strong movement learning foundation. The movement key experiences include the breadth of kinesthetic experiences that preschoolers need if they are to function with strength, balance, coordination, basic timing, and agility. The experiences also strengthen and extend many other important learning areas by involving young children in aural, visual, and tactile experiences; experiences requiring attention and concentration; and experiences requiring creativity, problem solving, language, planning, and decision-making. Indeed, the movement key experiences are the most important part of the High/Scope *Education Through Movement— Building the Foundation* active learning process described in this book.

Chart 1.1

High/Scope Preschool Key Experiences in Movement, by Category

Engaging the Learner	Enabling the Learner	Extending the Learner
Acting upon movement directions	Moving in nonlocomotor ways	Expressing creativity in movement
Describing movement	Moving in locomotor ways	Feeling and expressing steady beat
	Moving with objects	Moving in sequences to a common beat

In subsequent chapters, the eight key experiences will be described in detail in relation to the three broad categories mentioned earlier: **engaging, enabling, and extending** the learner. Chapter 2 explores the first two key experiences, which fall within the category **engaging the learner:**

- **Acting upon movement directions**—the child understands and responds to verbal directions, imitates accurately, and becomes familiar with movements through another person's hands-on guidance.

- **Describing movement**—the child identifies and talks about a movement being performed, plans the movement before it occurs, recalls the movement after doing it, and uses the learner SAY & DO process.

Chapter 3 explores the next three key experiences that fall within the **enabling the learner** category and that involve three major types of movement:

- **Moving in nonlocomotor ways**—the child performs movements in personal space (i.e., without moving around). These experiences involve movements of the upper and lower body in any non-weightbearing position and movements of the body while standing that do not result in transferring weight from one foot to the other foot. Thus the child becomes aware of how the body can move while anchored (i.e., not moving through space). Examples of this experience include pounding with fists on the legs or on the floor while sitting; shaking both hands in front of the body or in other places around the body; swinging the arms while standing or the legs while sitting or lying down; twisting the arms, legs, trunk (at the waist); bending and straightening the arms, legs, or trunk.

These children and their teacher, Phyllis, are exploring ways to move their feet while remaining on their carpet squares. Preschoolers need lots of these kinds of kinesthetic movement experiences in personal space.

- **Moving in locomotor ways**—the child performs basic locomotor skills such as walking and jumping where there is a non-anchored weight transfer. By using an appropriate sequence for developing these skills, the child becomes more aware of how the body can move in personal space and can travel about in general space.

- **Moving with objects**—the child uses objects with both nonlocomotor and locomotor movement. Examples of this experience include throwing, catching, kicking, and striking a ball; moving with scarves, ribbons, rhythm sticks, bobbins, beanbags, and paper plates.

Chapter 4, explores the three key experiences that are grouped under the **extending the learner** category:

This preschooler (far right) is leading steady beat with both hands. Using two hands to perform the same action is easier for preschoolers than using one hand alone. Alternating hands is the most difficult hand action for preschoolers.

- **Expressing creativity in movement**—the child extends movement activities through problem solving, guided exploration, and representation. The goal of this key experience is to have children become comfortable using their own ideas for nonlocomotor and locomotor movement and movement with objects in creative ways.

- **Feeling and expressing steady beat**—the child becomes aware of and moves to the beat of a rhyme, song, or instrumental musical selection. The goal of this key experience is to have children achieve **basic timing** as they independently feel, express, and keep the steady beat in nonlocomotor ways and to be able to walk to the beat, thus achieving **steady beat competence.**

- **Moving in sequences to a common beat**—the child develops body coordination, a process described as **levels of beat coordination.** This sequence helps young children develop the movement coordination needed to move with a partner or a group—all using the same beat as they move together.

Movement Core

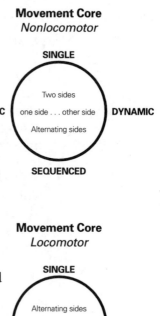

The **movement core,** illustrated in the diagrams at right, is intended as a summary of the motor development base for purposeful movement for all ages in the High/Scope *Education Through Movement—Building the Foundation* program. Aspects of the **movement core** have been modified to meet the needs of young children and will be referred to throughout this book. Note that one of the **movement core** diagrams is labeled "nonlocomotor" and the other is labeled "locomotor." The text inside the circle of each diagram refers to the way the body can be organized for purposeful movement. For any age, "two sides" is the easiest when using nonlocomotor movement, while "alternating" is easiest when using locomotor movement. In other words, movement complexity is illustrated in this diagram from top to bottom— with the easiest movement at the top of the diagram and the more complex at the bottom. As you introduce movement activities to young children, this simple-to-more-complex way of moving should be kept in mind.

The words placed around the circle of each **movement core** diagram refer to the ways that the body executes purposeful movement. A single movement is easier than a sequenced movement to organize, and a static movement is easier than a dynamic movement. The terms used in the diagram are defined as follows:

- **Two sides** refers to two corresponding parts of the body (e.g., both arms, legs, hands, elbows) moving in the same way at the same time. Examples would be patting the head with both hands, twisting both arms, shaking both hands, bending and straightening both legs. When you encourage children to move two sides in nonlocomotor movement, you are introducing the easiest way of organizing body movements in motor development.

- **One side...other side** refers to movement of one of the two arms, legs, or hands without the other one moving. Twisting one arm several times or hopping on one foot several times are one-sided movements. The movement should then be repeated on the other side *alone*. It is important to suggest that children use the "other" side so that they work the part of the brain that controls such movements and so you can discover if the child is more comfortable using that side.

- **Alternating** refers to two corresponding body parts taking turns in moving (one side moving immediately after the other side). Walking, in which one leg at a time takes a step, is an example of alternating movement, as is galloping, performed with uneven timing. Patting one hand on the knee one time and then patting the other hand on the other knee one time, and so on, is another example. While alternating is the easiest *locomotor* movement, it is the most difficult *nonlocomotor* movement to coordinate.

- **Static** refers to movement that pauses or is held still. When demonstrating a static movement, you might place both hands on your shoulders and then pause, with hands remaining on the shoulders, to make it easy for children to copy the movement. Static movement can also be initiated with verbal suggestions: "Try putting both hands on your knees." (Pause.) "Now try patting your knees softly" (the patting movement is a dynamic movement, which is defined next).

- **Dynamic** refers to movement that continues without pausing, requiring children to track the movements. Patting the shoulders repeatedly is a dynamic movement, as is walking. Dynamic movement can involve **two sides** (swinging both arms) or **one side...other side** (swinging one arm repeatedly, then the other arm) or **alternating sides.**

- **Single** refers to one movement held or one movement repeated (patting knees or stepping). If a child can say one word with each motion ("KNEES, KNEES, KNEES, KNEES," or "STEP, STEP, STEP, STEP") the movement is single; it has only one part that is purposeful.

- **Sequenced** refers to two or more different movements joined together. Touching knees, then shoulders is a sequenced movement because both movements are purposeful. Two or more words accompany the movement ("KNEES, SHOULDERS; KNEES SHOULDERS" or "UP, DOWN; UP, DOWN"). It is the *purposeful* part of the movement that makes it **single** or **sequenced.**

Teaching Model

The ease with which children, young people, or adults grasp movement activities or interpret directions often depends on the way the activities or directions are presented to them—on whether the teacher's presentation is based on the **teaching model** and the **movement core.**

The **teaching model** can be used to engage children in all types of enjoyable movement-based activities. For children to experience success, adults should be consistent in their approach and should be aware of the developmental levels of the children involved.

The **teaching model** has these three major components:

- **Separate**—demonstrate or tell or use hands-on guidance

- **Simplify**—begin with what is easy or manageable to learn

- **Facilitate**—engage children in action, thought, and language

> ### Chart 1.2
>
> *Education Through Movement Teaching Model*
>
> ---
>
> **Separate:** *Demonstrate*
>
>   or
>
>   *Tell*
>
>   or
>
>   *Use hands-on guidance*
>
> **Simplify:** *Begin with what is easy or manageable to learn.*
>
> **Facilitate:** *Engage children through action, thought, and language.*

Chart 1.2 provides a handy summary of the **teaching model.** Now, in the following sections, let's take a closer look at each of these components.

The "Separate" Component

This component involves initiating experiences or providing guidance by using only one mode of presentation at a time. Children absorb external information in three distinct ways that correspond to the following three modes of presentation.

- By **demonstration,** which means that the child must process the visual information in order to respond

- By **verbal (spoken) directions,** which means that the child must process the verbal information in order to respond

- By **hands-on guidance,** which means that the child must literally process the "felt" movement in order to respond

By choosing to **separate,** to use only one of these three presentation modes at a time, we enable children to focus on a single message. Combining one or more modes of presentation—explaining verbally while demonstrating, or explaining verbally while giving hands-on guidance, for example—often confuses the child because too much sensory input is provided.

I have found that using the **separate** strategy captures the child's attention and strengthens each movement learning experience. However, it is important to maintain an appropriate balance between the different modes of presentation— even for young children. Consider what each of the three modes involves:

- **Demonstration**. You should usually precede the demonstration with a simple statement that gains children's attention ("Watch and copy"). Then, without speaking, demonstrate a movement to be copied.

- **Verbal (spoken) directions.** You should usually precede your verbal instruction with a statement such as, "Please listen and follow these directions." This lets children know that important information is coming. Without demonstrating, offer children verbal directions about what to do. Because the move-

*This child leader is demonstrating the use of two sides as she extends both arms in front of her body for the adults and other children to copy. By only demonstrating she is using the **separate** method.*

ment is not demonstrated, the children will interpret the movement idea in a variety of ways. Watch for children who look to others for the interpretation. They are processing visually.

- **Hands-on guidance.** After gaining permission to touch the child, you might say, "I'm going to raise your arms up high." Then, without providing any more verbal information, raise the child's arms overhead. The hands-on assistance and the verbal message do not occur simultaneously. You could, however, raise the child's arms and then verbally describe what was just done.

These three modes of presentation are discussed further in Chapter 2 in the section dealing with the movement key experience *acting upon movement directions*. In that section a *series of movements for responding* are also described—these stages are designed to improve children's visual, aural, and tactile/kinesthetic understanding and perception. Please note, however, that the three separate presentation modes can and should be used when introducing any of the eight movement key experiences or any of the other High/Scope key experiences. Breaking the "show and tell" habit is worth the effort with regard to the key experiences because young children learn to listen, to watch, and to feel the movements.

The "Simplify" Component

This component involves beginning with what is easy or manageable to learn, so everyone can become immediately engaged in the learning process and experience success. When we simplify a movement experience, we begin with an activity or task that is fairly easy to do and that, based on our child observations, we believe all children can master. Perhaps we are considering introducing an important movement, coordination, or basic timing skill that we decide to initiate because we haven't seen children doing it. Let's say that we haven't seen children hopping, so we wish to introduce this experience. We realize that children need to balance on each foot in order to hop successfully, and we decide that our group of youngsters will be able to do this quite easily. Therefore, we begin by suggesting that the children try to balance on one foot; this is a **simplify** strategy—a static movement in the **movement core.** Another example: If we want children to use steady beat with a patting motion on their knees; we begin by having them place both their hands on their knees—a single, static movement—before undertaking the continuous patting movement. See Chart 1.3 for guidelines on judging the complexity of a movement.

The "Facilitate" Component

The first two components of the **teaching model** (**separate** and **simplify**) are strategies that we use in introducing movement activities. The third and last component of the **teaching model**—the **facilitate** strategy—concerns all the ways that we engage children through action, thought, and language as we support them in developing awareness and skills and constructing their own knowledge.

Chart 1.3

Guidelines Concerning Simple-to-Complex Tasks

In judging how easy or difficult a movement task is for young children, these are some guidelines to follow:

- Static movement (movement that pauses) is easier than dynamic movement (continuous movement).

- Movements that have endpoints against the body are easier to perceive than movements with endpoints away from the body.

- Movements of the upper body (nonlocomotor) are easier than the weight-bearing movements (locomotor).

- Gross-motor movements are easier than fine-motor movements.

- Movement without an object is easier than movement with an object.

- In nonlocomotor movement (movement with the body anchored, without weight transfer), for young children moving two sides simultaneously (corresponding body parts—arms, for example) is easier than moving just one side or alternating such movements.

- In locomotor movement (movement with the body not anchored, with foot patterns and weight transfer), for young children alternating movement (marching) is easier than two-sided movement (jumping) or one-sided movement (hopping).

- Single movements are easier than sequenced movements.

- Personal space (the area immediately around a person) is easier to manage than general space (the total movement area that is available).

We **facilitate** when we encourage and support children in initiating their own ideas and experiences. We **facilitate** when we give children time to explore movement activities and concepts on their own, to apply their existing understanding and skills to movement and other tasks. Asking children to talk about what they are going to do *(plan)*, supporting and encouraging them as they carry out their plans *(do)*, and then helping them to reflect on what they did *(recall or review)* are other ways we can **facilitate.**

Asking questions that provoke thought is another important way to **facilitate.** The types of questions you might ask or statements you might use can be organized as follows from most to least thought-provoking:

1. **Questions that have a yes/no or correct answer.** While this type of question is useful on occasion, it should not be used exclusively. Examples: "Where did we put our hands [legs]? Did they get there at the same time?" "Did you go down the slide fast?" "Did you and Jeffrey jump together?" These types of questions are the least thought-provoking because the child can give a simple "yes" or "no" answer.

2. **Questions that are thought-provoking because students are making a choice between or among various movement concepts.** Examples: "Did you move your arms quickly or slowly? Did your arms move at the same time or one at a time?" "When you patted your knees, were they big pats or little pats?" Now the child makes a choice between two possibilities—a little more thought-provoking.

3. **Questions that have no specific correct answer or that require a choice between or among solutions given (*divergent* questions).** Such questions or statements require the children to think through what they have done. Examples: Lucinda has been the leader during large-group time. Mac, the adult, says, "Let's tell Lucinda something about the way she had us move" or "What did we have to do when we galloped slower?" or "How did you travel to the planning table?" or "Tell me how you moved across the room."

*Katy has been exploring movement with paper bags filled with poly-fiberfill. Her teacher has asked Katy to talk about her movements, thus using the **facilitate** component of the **teaching model.***

Active Learning Strategies for Movement

Adults working with young children, indeed adults working with students of *any* age, should not be *directors* of children's activities or *dispensers* of information. Instead, in keeping with the High/Scope educational philosophy, we urge you to adopt active learning strategies for introducing and supporting children's movement key experiences. (See the sidebar on page 28 for specific information on introducing the movement key experiences to young children.)

In an active learning setting we not only initiate ideas but also recognize opportunities (through careful child observation) for supporting and extending ideas initiated by children. Because "to do is to understand," in active learning settings children are encouraged to make their own choices and decisions, to share their ideas, to assist one another, and to talk about their experiences. We help children reflect on what they have done, which in our case brings their purposeful movements to an appropriate level of awareness and understanding.

Brian is exploring ways to toss and catch this ball. He is also beginning to talk about his experiences.

The following program elements are based on the High/Scope active learning approach and have been modified to fit the needs of High/Scope's *Education Through Movement—Building the Foundation* program for young children:

- Initiation by adults and children

- Exploration of purposeful movement

- Choices and planning by children

- Language listened to and supplied

- Facilitation and reflection

- Support from adults and peers

Initiation by Adults and Children

Initiation of ideas by both adults and children is critical to successful learning. When children are free to offer their suggestions and ideas along with the adult, they generally will maintain a high level of interest in an activity. Furthermore, you will discover that ideas that are mutually generated by adults and children far surpass those generated solely by adults.

Exploration of Purposeful Movement

When young children have lots of opportunities to explore and work with movement ideas and activities, they will develop a true understanding of and ability to apply purposeful movement. Also, children truly enjoy exploring movements initiated by an adult, another child, or themselves. Providing appropriate adult encouragement and support not only enables young children to learn about movement but also ensures the success of their many movement ideas and experiences.

Choices and Planning by Children

Making choices and planning is an integral part of the daily routine in the High/Scope Curriculum. In addition to a daily **planning time-work time-recall time sequence,** children have numerous other opportunities to make choices and decisions. Many of these choices involve movement-related activities: how to go down the slide, how to move around the large-group-time circle, which body part to pat to the steady beat, how to move over to a small group. Indeed, an active learning environment opens the door to all kinds of enjoyable and exciting movement experiences for children.

Language Listened To and Supplied

Throughout the High/Scope daily routine, conversations occur freely and spontaneously among children and between adults and children. Many of these conversations are about movement-related topics. Throughout the day, children are constantly listening to language and are encouraged to supply language—talking about what they are doing and thinking, and often how they are moving. An important role for the adult is to reinforce with language many of the things children choose to do—including how they move about. This enables children to develop not only movement abilities but also cognitive understanding of what their bodies are doing. Adults ask questions that do not intrude but instead serve to stimulate children's thinking and problem solving.

How to Introduce the Movement Key Experiences to Young Children

First, read through this book to obtain an overview of the concepts presented. Following this review, we recommend that you become comfortable with the two key experiences that fall in the category of **engaging the learner** *(acting upon movement directions* and *describing movement)*. The next three key experiences—*moving in nonlocomotor ways, moving in locomotor ways,* and *moving with objects*—deal with **enabling the learner** and should be introduced together. Imagine children being involved in these three experiences in a continuous ebb-and-flow pattern that includes the other key experiences, rather than in a preordained, separate movement sequence. The three key experiences dealing with **extending the learner** are also part of this fluid learning process. For example, *expressing creativity in movement* can involve experiences that fall under the **engaging the learner** category. This is a good key experience to introduce when the children are comfortable with movement, have formed a movement vocabulary, and understand what their bodies can do. *Feeling and expressing steady beat* lays the foundation for moving with others to a common beat and therefore needs to be reinforced with very simple movements (so it fits well with the three key experiences under **enabling the learner**). Also, *moving in sequences to a common beat* can be useful in extending the *feeling and expressing steady beat* key experience. Children will learn how to move with a partner or in a group, with or without music. *Moving in sequences to a common beat* must be synchronized with other key experiences or with music. You can introduce this action by "adding it on" to some of the other experiences the children have already engaged in.

Facilitation and Reflection

Focusing on movement-related learning is easy in a High/Scope classroom, center, or home. For example, after children have participated actively in a task at work time, they can reflect on their movements at recall time, and the adult can facilitate their learning by asking relevant questions to extend and expand on the experience. Questions are best when they encourage children to continue to reflect on their experiences, to think back over the movements tried. As noted earlier, such **facilitation** is one of the three major components of the **teaching model** that guides the movement learning process.

Marisa and her friend Allison are copying each other's ways of walking. Each time either girl is the leader, she makes a new choice about her method of walking.

Support From Adults and Peers

A supportive learning environment is essential if we are to help children develop new skills, including those involving some form of movement, by building on their existing capabilities. Providing a positive, supportive atmosphere means realizing that we and the children are embarking together on an educational journey; each person brings something valuable to the journey. If we set a supportive tone in the preschool by offering appropriate encouragement and suggestions and by encouraging children to support one another, then the classroom becomes an exciting and comfortable place in which to learn.

Summary

The movement-based active learning process has four components:

- The eight key experiences in movement

- The movement core

- The teaching model

- The active learning strategies

Taken together, these four components can build a firm foundation from which we can support and extend children's purposeful movement experiences.

Engaging the Learner 2

Acting upon movement directions and *describing movement* are the two **movement key experiences** included under the **engaging the learner** category. They influence all aspects of young children's development. When children are actively engaged in the learning process, it means they are paying attention to what is occurring and are actually constructing their own knowledge. Children who are actively engaged in a movement experience are able to (1) understand what is requested of them, (2) understand what their bodies are doing, and (3) understand how to plan what they are going to do, how to describe it, and how to recall it.

Engaging children in this manner is a challenging task for us because children must be supported and challenged at *their* level of development and understanding. Moreover, we need to encourage children to take initiative, make choices and decisions, and express their thoughts and intentions. When engaging in the two movement key experiences highlighted in this chapter, children will achieve the following goals: (1) increased visual, auditory, and tactile perception, (2) increased attention span and concentration, (3) increased movement awareness, and (4) increased ability to understand and talk about movement experiences. By using the **separate, simplify,** and **facilitate** components of the **teaching model** as well as the strategies of the **movement core,** we will be able to support children as they acquire and strengthen these important skills and abilities. It is important to consider two key points when working with young children to introduce successfully these and related movement key experiences:

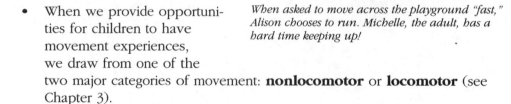

When asked to move across the playground "fast," Alison chooses to run. Michelle, the adult, has a hard time keeping up!

- When we provide opportunities for children to have movement experiences, we draw from one of the two major categories of movement: **nonlocomotor** or **locomotor** (see Chapter 3).

- When we choose to introduce a movement that is age-appropriate and new to the children we are working with, we must decide how to simplify it to assure their success and how to present it either visually, verbally, or with hands-on guidance.

In this chapter we explore the essential elements for insuring that young children will be successful and thus become more confident and comfortable when engaging in the two key experiences under the **engaging the learner** category. First, lets's examine what's needed for experiencing success with the *acting upon movement direction* key experience.

Key Experience:
Acting Upon Movement Directions

How do we help children understand what we want them to do when we, or another child, give them verbal directions? Do we expect them to immediately comprehend such directions? How do we help children understand and then respond to our visual movement demonstrations or to the movement demonstrations of other children? If we provide hands-on guidance to help a child recognize steady beat by taking his arms and doing the movement with him—will he be able to understand and respect the movement? These questions pinpoint many of the problems children experience while developing motor skills, which may be the result of their inability to understand verbal directions (an aural processing problem), to understand visually demonstrated directions (a visual processing problem), or to understand and respond to movement presented with "hands-on guidance" (a tactile/kinesthetic processing problem).

Erin has been encouraged to demonstrate, without talking, movements for the other children and the adult to copy.

When children play with other children and adults, they have many opportunities to think about and carry out movement ideas, to follow others' directions, to copy what others are doing, and to move about while holding someone else's hands. This is the natural way children learn about movement in early childhood.

Drawing on these naturally occurring early learning situations, we can introduce simple movements using the *acting upon movement directions* key experience. These movements will gradually become more complex but will still be appropriate for young children. Let us consider several guidelines for introducing movement directions to young children in this manner.

Guidelines for Supporting Young Children as They Act Upon Movement Directions

These guidelines are suggestions only. You may discover variations of them that work better for you. Remember that the desired end result is to help children increase their attention span and be successful in acting upon movement directions presented verbally, by demonstration, or by hands-on guidance.

1. **Use only one presentation method at a time.** According to the **separate** strategy of the **teaching model,** either *demonstrate,* or *use verbal directions,* or *use hands-on guidance.* Watching an adult who is talking and demonstrating simultaneously requires young children to integrate too much information. Thus, either *describing verbally* or *demonstrating physically* will best capture the child's attention. This is true also when only *hands-on guidance* is employed, because the child can "feel" the movement; no words are necessary. (When children are the leaders, it probably will be easier for them to demonstrate or to give hands-on guidance than to give verbal directions.) Although adults who are accustomed to talking while demonstrating may find this habit difficult to break, the results are worth the effort. These methods are described in detail later in this chapter.

2. **Begin with movements while seated.** The seated position is easier for children to use when responding to movement directions. Also greater numbers of lower-body movements are possible.

3. **Keep the presentation simple.** When providing verbal directions, adults should keep the number of words used to a minimum. Pause after *each* direction is given. Keep in mind the **movement core** and always begin with movements that are symmetrical on both sides (e.g., both hands on the knees). The section on "Stages of Movement for Responding (Aural, Visual and Tactile/Kinesthetic Processing)," presented later in this chapter, explains the simple to more complex movements that are suitable for young children.

4. **Use static movements before dynamic movements.** Pause after each single movement, thus giving children time to respond. *Slow* dynamic movement (continuous movement) must be continually watched and tracked by the followers, so try this kind of movement only when children are comfortable copying static movement and are able to attend for a longer period of time. Dynamic movements are discussed in more detail in Chapter 3, "Enabling the Learner," and Chapter 4, "Extending the Learner."

5. **Be certain all the children can easily see and hear either you or the child leader.** If your group is sitting in a circle, for example, the children on either side of the leader may need to move in order to see clearly.

6. **Present movements that, in your judgment, all the children will be able to do successfully.** Carefully observe the children to see if they all

are successful. If some of them are struggling, look to see if they are attending to the task; also consider whether the task may be too difficult (or too easy) or whether the directions have not been presented clearly.

7. **Make the movements age-appropriate.** Younger children can best understand "on-the-body" movements, for example, using their hands to touch the head, shoulders, or toes.

8. **Move slowly.** The ability of the group should dictate how quickly you can move from one verbal, visual, or hands-on direction to another. Moving too quickly negates the reason for involving children in this key experience.

9. **Avoid giving directions that indicate right or left.** Until second grade or later, avoid requiring movements that use specific "right" or "left" sides. Allow each child to determine which side to use. You can say, for example, "one side" then "other side," or "first side" then "second side."

10. **Have fun with the children.** We need to think of ourselves as *partners* with children in the learning process. Movement experiences should not be thought of as drill-and-practice sessions but as enjoyable, fun-filled experiences. Children respond best when they enjoy what they are doing.

11. **Sing the verbal directions on random pitches.** Often children pay more attention to the sung versus the verbal suggestion. You will notice that children will be eager to sing the suggestions along with you.

12. **Have the children be the leaders of the group.** Give children opportunities to be leaders for the entire group. Besides empowering the children, being a leader strengthens their awareness and knowledge of movement experiences and improves their vocabulary. Also, we can learn a great deal about the children in our care when the leadership role is turned over to them. When children lead, they will settle in to use purposeful movement. They will realize that "off-the-wall" movements cannot be copied.

13. **After introducing a more difficult stage of movement (the stages are described next) keep returning to the easier ones.**

These 13 guidelines should help you devise enjoyable games and activities for young children. We are also guided by the four **stages of movement for responding** that young children are able to process aurally, visually, or tactile/kinesthetically as they are *acting upon movement directions.*

Stages of Movement for Responding (Aural, Visual, and Hands-on Guidance)

For young children, there are essentially four stages or levels of difficulty involved in the key experience *acting upon movement directions.* These stages are described in the following pages and are listed in Chart 2.1. Many of the activities described later in this chapter fall in the first stage, **single symmetrical**

Chart 2.1

Stages of Movement for Responding (Visual, Aural, and Tactile/Kinesthetic Processing) for Young Children

Stage 1: Single symmetrical movements

SAME or DIFFERENT * SAME, AT THE SAME TIME

Leader uses corresponding body parts to do a single movement, ending in the same place, and pauses for children's response.

Stage 2: Single alternating movements

SAME or DIFFERENT * SAME, ONE SIDE AT A TIME

Leader moves one body part, children respond; leader does identical movement with corresponding body part, children respond (no right/left, mirroring, or reversal).

Stage 3: Single asymmetrical movements

SAME or DIFFERENT * DIFFERENT, AT THE SAME TIME

Leader uses corresponding body parts to do different movements at the same time and pauses for children's response.

Stage 4: Single alternating asymmetrical movements

SAME or DIFFERENT * DIFFERENT, ONE SIDE AT A TIME

Leader moves one body part, children respond; leader moves corresponding body parts to different location, children respond.

movements. Start at this first stage and proceed "up the ladder," trying each stage to see if your children can be successful, but returning often to the easier stages for quick success. **You do not need to wait for all children to succeed at one stage before trying another.** Several of these terms are defined in Chapter 1, and a summary is provided in Chart 2.2, "Terms Used in Stages of Movement for Responding." Please review this information before continuing.

Stage 1

SINGLE SYMMETRICAL MOVEMENTS. At this stage, which is the easiest for any learner, **the child moves paired body parts (e.g., both hands) in a single symmetrical movement, which is then held static and identified. Both hands pause at the same location on the body (e.g., at the waist) or in the same location away from the body (e.g., out to the sides). The child's hands can start their movement from the same position (e.g., from both being on the shoulders) or from *different* positions (e.g., from one hand being on a shoulder and the other hand being on the head).** Chart 2.3 summarizes the Stage 1 movement possibilities. The single symmetrical movement, if performed with both legs, might be done while lying down or seated; there are only a few symmetrical leg movements that can be done while standing.

Using one of the three recommended presentation methods listed in guideline 1, page 34, the Stage 1 movement response activity might go like this:

- **Verbal directions (aural processing)**—Say or sing, without demonstrating, "Put your hands on your knees" or "Put your hands on your head." Eventually, when it is clear to children that the hands are doing the moving, you might shorten the verbal directions to "on your knees" and "on your head." It is important that directions be brief for young children, so their attention does not lapse before the directions are finished. When the children themselves lead the movements, you will be able to assess the language development of each leader by the verbal directions given. *Note:* Don't forget you can also sing directions using random pitches.

- **Demonstration (visual processing)**—Demonstrate movement that stops with both hands on the same body location or in the same position away from the body. Place both hands on your shoulders, then *without speaking,* move both hands to your knees (the hands began in the same place—

Chart 2.2

Terms Used in Stages of Movement for Responding

Static movement—A purposeful movement that pauses, or is held still, to allow children to respond.

Dynamic movement—A movement or sequence of movements that continues without pausing, requiring children to track the movement(s).

Single movement—Only *one* purposeful movement, performed and held static for children to respond. With dynamic movement, the one movement is performed over and over again.

Sequenced movement—Two different purposeful movements joined together, with each one held static to give children time to repeat each movement before the sequence is repeated. With dynamic movement, after the second movement ends, the sequence repeats several times.

Symmetrical movement—Movement in which two corresponding body parts move at once, ending up in the same location (e.g., both hands move to the top of the head).

Asymmetrical movement—Movement in which two corresponding or two different body parts move, ending up in different locations (e.g., both hands move, one ending up on the knee and one ending up at the waist; or one elbow moves to the knee and one hand moves to the shoulder).

Alternating movement—Two corresponding body parts take turns moving (e.g., one foot moves, then the other foot moves).

Chart 2.3

Stage 1: Single Symmetrical Movements

Movement begins	*Movement goes*
	TO SAME POSITION, AT SAME TIME
SAME	TO NEW POSITION, ONE AT A TIME
DIFFERENT	TO DIFFERENT POSITION, AT SAME TIME
	TO DIFFERENT POSITION, ONE AT A TIME

shoulders—and moved to the *new* place —knees—*at the same time).* The two hands could also begin in *different* places (e.g., head and shoulder) and move to a *new* place (knees) *at the same time.* After children have copied your first movement, which you have given from a seated position, proceed by straightening both legs in front of your body and then bending both knees. Children can also lead in demonstrating movements in this way for their classmates.

- **Hands-on guidance (tactile/kines-thetic processing)**—*Without talking,* move the child's hands to his or her head, and then stop. Then move them to a position straight in front of the child's body. You might ask the child the name of the body location, or the name of the position, where the hands stopped. *Note:* Be sure to first ask children's permission before touching them.

The simplest direction for children to follow visually is one in which the adult demonstrates a single movement.

Phyllis is demonstrating for the children how to place a pumpkin ball on their heads. Her single movement using both hands is the easiest for preschoolers to follow.

Stage 2

SINGLE ALTERNATING MOVEMENTS. At this stage, **the child moves one body part (hand, arm, finger, etc.) to a certain location (to the head, or to the chin, or to the same-side knee) and then moves the corresponding body part (the other hand) to the same (or corresponding) body location.** This stage is slightly more complex because only one side of the child's body moves at a time. In copying the leader, the child does not need to use the "correct" hand (i.e., the right if the leader used right, or the left if mirroring the leader's right-hand use). Most children will use their preferred side first. The hands begin from the same position (e.g., from both being at the sides, or both being on the shoulders, or both being on the head) and *end up* in a new location (knees or out in front), moving one at a time.

Chart 2.4 summarizes the Stage 2 movement possibilities. This is how the Stage 2 directions might be presented in a movement response game:

- **Verbal directions (aural processing)**—Give verbal or sung directions without demonstrating: "Put one hand on your shoulder." Wait for children to respond, then go on: "Put the other hand on your shoulder." Children responding to these two directions usually end up with one hand on each shoulder, but if a child ends up with both hands on the same shoulder, this is another possible interpretation. Of course, there are various ways to phrase the hand-shoulder directions.

- **Demonstration (visual processing)**—Start with both hands in the same location, on your head. Move *one* hand to your waist, and wait for the children to copy. Then move your *other* hand to your waist and wait for the children to copy. Again, children can choose whichever hand they prefer as their "starting hand." Success depends on the hands arriving at the new location, not on which hand arrives first.

- **Hands-on guidance (tactile/kinesthetic processing)**—Move the child's hands *one at a time,* without speaking during the movement. For example, take Jack's hand from his knee and place it at his waist. Then take Jack's other hand from his knee and also place it at his waist. (When working with special populations, you might have to verbally identify the placement or describe the movement in addition to hands-on guid-

---

Chart 2.4

Stage 2: Single Alternating Movements

Movement begins	Movement goes
	TO SAME POSITION, AT SAME TIME
SAME ⟶	TO NEW POSITION, ONE AT A TIME
DIFFERENT	TO DIFFERENT POSITION, AT SAME TIME
	TO DIFFERENT POSITION, ONE AT A TIME

ance but not at the same time.) Finally, put both of Jack's hands back on his knees and see if he can replicate the movement without your hands-on assistance. This type of hands-on guidance can also be done when children work as partners, with one child leading the other as a "puppet."

Jennifer, the adult in the classroom, is demonstrating a movement of only one hand. As is often the case, the children are looking at other children to copy rather than the adult in the classroom.

Stage 3

SINGLE ASYMMETRICAL MOVEMENTS. At this stage, **the child begins with both hands (or elbows, or fingers, etc.) on his or her head (or on the chin, or on the ears, etc.) and moves both hands *at the same time,* with one ending on the waist and one ending on the knees.** This stage is more complex because the child's corresponding body parts move to different locations. This is movement beginning in the same place and going to *different* places at the same time when following visually, and one at a time when responding to verbal directions. Chart 2.5 summarizes the Stage 3 movement possibilities. Notice that the chart shows Stage 3 movement also *starting in different places* and *going to different places,* for example, the hands begin on the head and shoulders and end on the waist and knees. Since this movement is more difficult for young children to respond to, we do not discuss these types of presentations in this book. It is easier for young children to begin by touching the same location (head), then a different location (waist and knee), and then a new location (shoulders).

This is how the Stage 3 directions might be presented in a movement response game:

Jennifer again uses the demonstration method as she places her two hands in different positions for the children to copy.

- **Verbal directions (aural processing)**—Because verbal directions cannot be given for two *different* locations at once, they must be given in two steps; say or sing, *without demonstrating,* "Move *one* hand to your shoulder," wait for a response, and then say or sing "Move the *other* hand down to your side." If children are not listening carefully, you will notice some of them moving the same hand twice, first to the shoulder, then to the side. Very young children may not understand the concept of "one hand" and then "the other hand," so the demonstration is easier for them.

- **Demonstration (visual processing)**—Beginning with both hands on your head, move both hands *at the same time,* but to two different positions, such as one moving to the waist and one moving to the shoulder.

- **Hands-on guidance (tactile/kinesthetic processing)**—Begin by placing both of the child's hands on his or her chin. Then simultaneously move one hand to the top of the child's head and the other hand to the

---

Chart 2.5

Stage 3: Single Asymmetrical Movements

Movement begins	Movement goes
	TO SAME POSITION, AT SAME TIME
SAME	TO NEW POSITION, ONE AT A TIME
DIFFERENT	TO DIFFERENT POSITION, AT SAME TIME
	TO DIFFERENT POSITION, ONE AT A TIME

child's shoulder. You can then ask the child to identify the two placements, or you can describe what you just did. Then put the child's hands back on the chin and suggest that the child try to repeat the single asymmetrical movement.

Stage 4

SINGLE ALTERNATING ASYMMETRICAL MOVEMENTS. At this stage, **the child moves one body part (e.g., a hand) on one side of the body from one location to another (e.g., from the head to the knee) and then moves the corresponding body part located in a different position (at the waist) on the other side of the body to a different location (e.g., moves the other hand from the waist to the foot). The child's two hands could also have started from the same place (e.g., both from the waist) and moved, one at a time, to different locations (e.g., one to the knee and the other to the foot).** Chart 2.6 summarizes the Stage 4 movement possibilities. This stage is more complex because the corresponding movement of body parts begin in *different* places, thus requiring the child to recognize which part is being designated to move first (e.g., "Move the hand that is on the head") and which part is being designated to move second. At this stage, the part to be moved is not identified as right or left, however; neither is the child expected to mirror or reverse the side the leader uses. In this situation, children must be paying close attention in order to move the designated body part. This is how Stage 4 movement directions can be presented:

- **Verbal directions (aural processing)**—Start with children having one hand on their ear and the other on top of their head, and say or sing "Move the hand that is on your ear out to the side. Now move the hand that is on top of your head to your foot." From this Stage 4 movement, you can go on to another Stage 4 movement or go back to a simpler stage. If you choose Stages 2 or 3, the wording becomes "one hand" and "the other hand." If you choose Stage 1, the wording becomes "both hands."

- **Demonstration (visual processing)**—Begin with your arms in different locations—one arm up and the other arm down. Move the "down" hand to your head, then move the "up" hand to your waist. Children copy each

---

Chart 2.6

Stage 4: Single Alternating Asymmetrical Movements

Movement begins	Movement goes
	TO SAME POSITION, AT SAME TIME
SAME	TO NEW POSITION, ONE AT A TIME
DIFFERENT	TO DIFFERENT POSITION, AT SAME TIME
	TO DIFFERENT POSITION, ONE AT A TIME

single movement before the next is shown. From this Stage 4 movement you can go to a Stage 1 movement, the easiest, or to Stages 2 or 3.

- **Hands-on guidance (tactile/kinesthetic processing)**—Begin with the child having one hand on the head and one on the shoulder. Move the child's hand from the head to the waist, and then ask which hand was moved ("the one from the head or the one from the shoulder?"). Then move the hand from the shoulder so it is extended out in front of the body, and ask the child to identify which hand moved that time.

Young children who have played movement response games with their parents and caregivers will be quite secure with Stages 1–4 when they enter kindergarten. Since these games are not played as often today, you should provide lots of opportunities for young children to build these abilities. *Work among the four stages, returning often to the beginning ones.* Don't forget to have children lead.

Once you understand the three recommended methods of introducing the *acting upon movement directions* key experience and are aware of the **four stages of movement** appropriate for young children, you are ready to consider some specific strategies and activities for introducing this important movement key experience.

Using Verbal Directions (Aural Processing)

It's large-group time in the preschool and the children are seated. Grace, one of the adults, says to the children, "Please listen and follow my directions. Put your hands on your chest." Grace waits for the children to respond and then continues, "Put your hands on your feet. Put your hands over your head. Put your legs out straight." Grace pauses after each direction to give the children time to respond. Grace then asks Caitlin, to be the leader by saying to her "Where shall we put our hands next?" Caitlin responds, "On our knees."

Notice that in this scenario Grace and Caitlin use only verbal directions. Let's look at some ways to give verbal directions that improve children's ability to concentrate on listening (aural responding).

The simplest aural responding occurs when the adult (or child) requests a *single* movement and one that requires action by both sides of the body in a symmetrical fashion. For example, children might be asked to put both hands on the same body part or both hands up in the air. As children are provided with these and similar verbal directions, watch for any children who may seem confused or who may be looking around to see what other children are doing. If a child is imitating and not responding by listening, try to find a time when it is appropriate to give verbal directions just to that child. Another strategy would be to say "Amanda, can you put your hands on your head? Justin, hands on your knees, please."

 ### Suggested Activities—Using Verbal Directions (Aural Processing)

1. Use this movement warm-up activity for large-group time. Present it by using either the *verbal direction* or *description* method. Start off by saying, *without demonstrating,* "Let's shake both hands in front of us. Let's shake them up high. Can you find another place to shake them? Where did you shake your hands, Ilana? Zongping? Kerry? Can you open your hands and stretch your fingers? Now let's curl our fingers. Can you wiggle your fingers on your head? Can you wiggle your fingers on your knees? Can you wiggle your fingers like the spider going up the water spout?" Then lead the children in the game "Eensy, Beensy Spider," after which you can introduce other large-group activities, *frequently asking individual children to provide the suggestions.*

2. The children are outside on the playground. Again using the *verbal description* method, begin a sequence of instructions: "Please listen carefully. First walk over to the slide, touch the slide with your elbows, and walk back." Before the children begin, have them recall the directions by asking them "What are you going to do first? How are you going to touch the slide? What are you going to do last?" Then say "Go." Other activities you could suggest include crawling through an object, walking backward to an object, or climbing over an object. *Also, encourage individual children to make some suggestions about how to move.*

3. Say to your preschoolers "Look around the room. Can you find something red?" After the children look about the room and locate a red object, say "Everyone walk to a red object and touch it." (Remind them that when they move about they should not come in contact with other children.) Repeat this activity using other colors. You might want to begin with only some members of the group moving. Instead of objects of a specified color, you could ask the children to locate objects of various sizes or shapes that you have placed around the room. You can also have the children touch the object or shape with a specified body part. *Also, be sure to give children the opportunity to make suggestions.*

Using Visual Demonstration (Visual Processing)

It is planning time in the preschool. Before Mary (the adult) begins to solicit the morning plans from the children, she engages them in a short visual demonstration game. Mary says, "Please watch and do what I'm doing." Mary then puts both hands on her head and waits for the children to respond. Then she silently places her hands on her knees. Next she stretches her hands up and then down in front of her body. After some of the moves Mary asks, "Where did we put our hands?" Mary then encourages the children to be the leaders in demonstrating various movements.

We can't assume that preschoolers can copy movement accurately, even though this ability should have been part of children's natural play and interactions with parents or caregivers before they came to preschool. Adults working with preschool children should support the development of this important perceptual ability by giving children lots of opportunities to figure out what is being demonstrated or what they are seeing.

As with verbal directions, the simplest visual demonstration involves a *single* movement presented with *both sides* of the body doing the same thing—a **symmetrical movement** (both hands touching both knees, for example).

 Suggested Activities—Visual Demonstration (Visual Processing)

1. To start off a group activity with a visual demonstration movement game, sit so the children can see you clearly. You can, for example, move your hands away from your body, such as high or low, or move your legs apart or bring them together. After each movement, ask the children "Where did we put our hands [feet]?" Children can also be the leaders for this easy stage. You might move one hand to one part of your body (knee) and simultaneously move the other hand to a different part of the body (nose), first saying "Watch. This may be harder." Afterwards ask "Where are our hands now?" Then you might also move one hand at a time to a part of the body, such as moving one hand to your head. When the children have copied your movement, move your other hand to your head, thus making the movement predictable. After the children are experienced with this activity, individual children can be leaders.

2. At outside time, suggest the children stand in an area with enough space so that all can move their arms about comfortably, and do the following activity to help the children understand how to copy your position: "Watch and copy." Stand with your hands on your hips and with your feet far apart. Ask the children "What have I done with my hands and my feet? Did you put your hands on *your* hips and your feet far apart? Change your position by placing both your arms out to the side and putting your feet close together. Encourage the children to copy your position. Then ask them to tell where they have placed their arms and legs. After providing several examples, ask for volunteers to plan and lead the group in assuming additional positions (statue shapes, for example).

3. Children are at small-group time in the preschool. Suggest that children each take two beanbags (it helps to have all of the beanbags in one color). Lead the children by placing the two beanbags on specific parts of your body, such as your knees. Ask the children to copy what you did. Then place the beanbags on two other body parts, and have children copy again. Have one of the children make the next three movement choices. Use child volunteers until all who wish to lead have had a turn.

Using Hands-on Guidance (Tactile/Kinesthetic Processing)

It is large-group time in the preschool. The children are going to play "statues," and Jose, one of the adults, is going to be the statue maker. To start the activity, Jose places Juanita's hands on her shoulders and asks her to "freeze" in that position and to identify the body part being moved. While moving Juanita's hands, Jose does not speak. He is therefore using only one presentation method (hands-on guidance). To promote awareness, he asks Juanita, "Where did I place your hands?"

The hands-on guidance method through which the child acquires knowledge and understanding from touch (kinesthetic awareness) is particularly effective when children are having difficulty understanding a movement presented by the verbal or visual methods. The important thing to remember is not to talk to children while you are physically guiding them. Instead, complete the movement in silence and then ask questions about the movement to assess whether or not the children understand it. This technique is particularly useful for children with special needs or children for whom English is not the first language. (Be certain to gain permission from the child to use the hands-on guidance method and respect their feelings. Some children may be unwilling to participate in this exercise.) As with the two other methods, the simplest movements are most appropriate for the hands-on guidance method—those that are *symmetrical.*

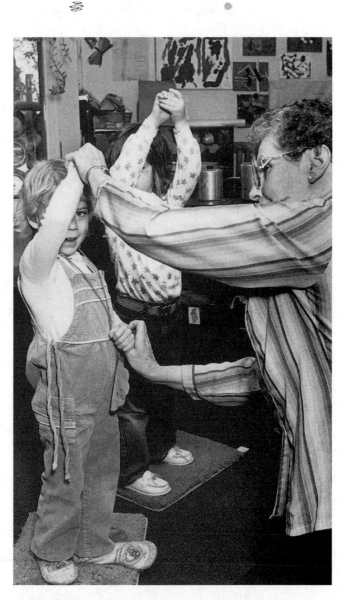

Phyllis is helping this child place her two hands in different places and then identify the placement. Phyllis is using hands-on guidance.

Suggested Activities—Hands-on Guidance
(Tactile/Kinesthetic Processing)

1. At large-group time in your preschool, you and the children can play "toy shop," with you or a child acting as the toy shop owner and the other children pretending to be wind-up toys. After the toy shop opens, the owner "winds up" a child. The child's arms are moved in some way, such as front and back. The child is asked to keep the movement going and to identify the movement.

2. Teachers and parents can play a game with children by placing a child's hands on various parts of the body or in various spatial positions or by placing the child's legs in various positions, such as straight out in front of the body. Ask the child to name the body part or position. Turn the game around and have the child be the leader while you join the other children as a participant.

3. Children can play the above game with a friend. One child guides the movements of the other child. The child can be lying down or seated or standing. The child who is the leader asks the other child to identify where the hands or feet have been placed or how they are moving. Make sure the children are gentle with each other and that they take turns being the leader.

4. Help children move their arms through the pattern of a geometric shape. For example, hold a child's two hands together and guide him or her in slowly tracing a shape. You can trace the pattern in the air, on the floor, on an object, or on the child's back. Ask the child to repeat the pattern in the air without your help. After children are experienced with this activity, let them take turns leading one another.

Methods of Having Children Assume Leadership

In early childhood it is important for a child to develop a sense of independence and initiative. Having children assume leadership roles while performing movement activities throughout all of the key experiences will help children develop such independent thinking. Many of the activities just described included suggestions that children also be leaders. Once children understand how to do the activity and understand the purpose of the activity, they will enjoy taking on the role of leader. One caution is that you make sure to give all children an equal opportunity to be leaders and not choose only the children who seem to be more capable or who always volunteer. Children who do not volunteer right away may think they need more time to understand the activity and may want to feel comfortable before volunteering. They may also be shy. You can ask non-volunteering children if they would like to make the next choice, but be ready to respect their wishes if they choose not to assume the leadership role. Here are some guidelines:

- Be certain the children understand the task you are asking them to lead.

- Ask children to suggest movement ideas of their own.

- Have children demonstrate a movement for everyone to copy.

Again, you'll notice throughout this book that suggestions are made for ways in which children can assume leadership roles. You will also find your own ways to encourage this. To have the children develop independence and initiative, *all* of the children need chances to assume the leadership function, not just a few.

At large-group time the children have asked to play the copycat game again. Their visual processing ability is being strengthened while they are thoroughly enjoying their game.

Appropriate times for using movement directions

In the preschool or child care setting, how do we incorporate into the daily schedule activities that strengthen children's listening skills, visual perception ability, and kinesthetic awareness of a tactile movement? Any time during the day is appropriate for activities that help children act upon movement directions. Specifically, these activities may be used throughout the day as a way of gaining the children's attention or of refocusing them before introducing the next block of time in the day, as part of large-group time, as a beginning or ending activity of the day, or as a brief break at any other time of the day.

How long should we do this type of activity at any one time? It is recommended that these activities be kept to short blocks of time; they certainly should not be extended beyond the children's ability to enjoy and attend to the task. Sometimes an activity is useful if only used for 30 seconds as a way of gaining the children's attention, as the alternative to saying "Everybody listen" or "Watch and copy" or "Shhhh." At other times we might continue for 2 or 3 minutes if the children are responding well and want to assume the role of leader.

Can these methods of helping children follow or understand what we want be extended beyond movement activities? They can be used in *all* aspects of your program. You should try to present directions in only one way at a time, i.e., tell the children, or show the children, or move the children. It will be more of a problem for children to follow directions if you are both showing and telling. If you want to demonstrate, first say "Watch me," or more specifically, "Watch what my arms are doing." If you want the children to listen, say "Please listen to these directions," or more specifically, "Please listen to these directions of how to move your arms." Afterwards, ask questions to assess whether or not the children understand.

Adding music

Recorded music (without lyrics) may be added at any time to the **four stages of movement** for the visual demonstration or hands-on guidance methods. (Lyrics can distract children from the task.) Depending on the ability of the group, movement changes should occur at the beginning of each 8-beat phrase of the music. You may also wish to use a familiar melody like "Are You Sleeping?" to sing along with a visual demonstration: Begin the movement first, such as swinging the arms, and then when children have joined in, begin to sing "Can you do this, can you do this?" or "Swing your arms, swing your arms. Swing our arms together, swing our arms together, just like me, just like me." Children can also suggest the movement and lead this activity. Just substitute one of their names for the word "me" and change the action word to suit what that child is doing.[1]

Summary of Acting Upon Movement Directions

To sum up, young children may find it difficult to act upon movement directions that are presented by combining verbal and visual or verbal and hands-on directions. When the methods are used separately, however, the children should be much more successful. Therefore, as you present activities in the subsequent key experiences, simplify your presentations by using only one of these methods and by starting off at the first of the four stages of movement for responding (aural, visual, and tactile/kinesthetic guidance) described in this chapter. To discover if the children understand what you are trying to convey, ask them pertinent questions after you have finished describing, demonstrating, or guiding. As you move into the more difficult stages, return often to the simpler stages so all the children can experience success. Keep in mind that you are a *partner* with the children in helping them achieve these basic abilities. Help them become independent in their thoughts and actions by having them assume leadership responsibilities.

---

[1]Additional suggestions for incorporating music into the **four stages of movement** for young children can be found in the booklet *Movement Plus Music* (Weikart, 1989), which identifies appropriate musical selections from the first four recordings in the companion *Rhythmically Moving* music series of nine recordings. For specific references to bands of music appropriate for the stages, see the *Guides to Rhythmically Moving 1–4* (Weikart & Carlton, 1996–1999). In addition, ideas for movement can be found in *Movement Plus Rhymes, Songs, & Singing Games* (Weikart, 1997) and *Movement in Steady Beat* (Weikart, 1990).

Key Experience: Describing Movement

Language is essential to achieving true understanding of movement concepts. If children can talk about their active learning experiences in movement, a new level of awareness of movement concepts is achieved and a cognitive-motor link is forged. As the wording implies, the key experience *describing movement* involves children in applying language to describe movements they perform, plan to perform, or have performed. Children as young as age 3 can use language in this way. For this to happen, of course, children not only need to experience movement but also to listen to others talk about their movements.

We understand that during their first 2 years of life children learn about their world through their senses, through the movement of their bodies, and by listening to others and exercising their developing language abilities. They explore, touch, grasp, move about. They develop motor skills as they learn to lift their heads, roll over, squirm and wiggle their way across the floor, get on their hands and knees and crawl, and stand upright and walk. Children develop language skills as they listen to others, learn to make sounds, pronounce single words, and put words together into phrases. By using language to describe movement, adults can help infants and toddlers as well as preschoolers develop a kinesthetic awareness of everyday movements—an awareness of what parts of

During their first 2 years of life, children learn through all their senses, through the movement of their bodies, and by listening to others and exercising their developing language abilities. They love to explore, as this little girl is doing, by touching and grasping as well as moving about.

the body can do together, separately, and in relation to other parts and to the surrounding space. For example, Josie, a caregiver, can describe to a child in her care what is happening during feeding and diapering; "I'm putting on your diaper now, Johnny. First I will fasten one side, and then I will fasten the other side." Josie can also label the child's actions: "Johnny, you are reaching for the rattle".

In discussing how preschoolers become actively engaged in learning by *describing movement,* we will explore the following five aspects of this key experience:

- **Listening to language about movement**—Comment on movement performed by children, so children not only receive nonjudgmental recognition but also hear descriptive language for their movement.

- **Talking about movement while doing it**—Engage children by posing movement problems that lead them to talk about their movement as they are doing it.

- **Planning movement before doing it**—Engage children by asking them to think about and describe how they plan to move.

- **Recalling movement after completion**—Engage children by asking them to think about and describe movement already completed.

- **Learner SAY & DO**—Encourage children to link each single movement with a single descriptive word, so thought directs the movement; action, thought, and language are united.

In examining these five aspects of *describing movement,* we will be emphasizing the **facilitate** component of the **teaching model.** Adults become *facilitators* of children's learning. As we facilitate we need to keep in mind the desired results of *describing movement,* which are children's improved thinking ability and use of language.

In the sections that follow, each of these steps is described in terms of appropriate activities that can occur naturally in preschool and child care settings. These activities are based on the High/Scope Preschool Curriculum developmental approach and can be implemented easily in a variety of settings. Various scenarios are also provided to illustrate how you can introduce young children to the *describing movement* key experience.

The Importance of Listening To Language About Movement

It's work time in the preschool. Cressida and Valencia have dressed up in assorted clothing and now are holding hands and jumping around. Bonnie, one of the adults in the preschool, verbally describes the girls' jumping movements, mentioning that they are turning around as they jump and that both their feet are landing on the floor at the same time. Then the girls ask Bonnie to join them so all three can jump together.

As infants and toddlers roll over, squirm, crawl, and finally walk, they hear adults using *relevant* language to describe these early explorations of the world. Listening to the adult language, children begin to develop kinesthetic aware-ness—a sense of how body parts move together or separately, of how body parts are related to one another and to the surrounding environment. As children reach preschool age, we can continue to comment on their various movements: "Tim, I see you are jumping over puddles." "Kayla, you skipped all the way across the yard!" We can also begin to question children about movement in ways that encourage them to think more about what they are doing: "Brian, I see you're turning your arm around and around. What else are you doing? I'd like to do it with you."

Such an adult comment, well placed, can recognize a child's actions, provide the child with descriptive language, and provide a personally meaningful interaction between the adult and child. As with any technique or approach, however, com-menting on children's movements should not be over-used. Also, we should be careful to comment in ways that are relevant and understandable to children and to sound encouraging and supportive of the young child's movement explorations.

 ### Suggested Activities—Listening To Language About Movement

1. The children are on the playground. Eileen, the adult present, encourages the children to find different ways to go down the slide, but the children become so engaged in the activity they don't process or plan how they will go down the slide. Therefore, Eileen describes for each child all the ways she observes that child coming down the slide, and she mentions what was the same or different about each effort.

2. Children have been encouraged to march around the large-group-time cir-cle in different ways. They are marching to "Apat Apat" a selection from the *Rhythmically Moving 4* recording. As each child passes by Jerome, the adult, he says something to that child about the way he or she is march-ing. After all the children have explored ways to march, Jerome asks Herbie to be the leader. The other children eagerly follow Herbie. Jerome tells Herbie one thing about the way he marched and then asks the other children if they noticed anything else about Herbie's marching.

3. Children are playing statues. Each child assumes a statue position. Penny, the adult, goes from child to child, first giving information about the posi-tion of one body part (an arm) and then giving each child information about where she is going to move the body part. Penny describes what she is going to do before providing hands-on guidance.

Talking About Movement While Doing It

It's large-group time in the preschool. The children are sitting on the floor and they are moving their arms in many ways. Ofelia, their teacher, encourages the children to describe how they are moving their arms by asking "Will someone show us and tell us how they are moving their

arms?" Jane volunteers. When Jane finishes, Ofelia asks Jane a relevant question: "Jane, can you tell us some more about what your arms are doing?" Jane has only used a single word to describe her movement: "Swinging." Using complete sentences, Ofelia expands on what Jane has said: "Jane told us that she is swinging her arms. Where is she swinging her arms? Let's all try to swing our arms in front of our bodies the way Jane is swinging hers. Can someone show us another way to swing our arms? How else can we swing our arms?"

The important thing about this scenario is that preschool children are being asked to think about how they are moving (what they are doing) and to use language to describe their actions. They are becoming aware that their actions can be put into words (experiencing language concepts), are developing a basic understanding of how the body can move in space (experiencing spatial concepts), and are discovering how long it takes to complete such movements (experiencing time concepts). In addition, as children listen to more and more movement descriptions from others, they will become comfortable enough to begin providing and then expanding their own descriptions of how they are moving.

Our role in helping children develop good motor skills should be that of asking questions and making comments to increase children's awareness of what they are doing. For example, in the above scenario of children exploring what their arms can do, Ofelia, the teacher could extend the activity by asking "Are we moving our arms quickly or slowly?" With questions like these, both the type of movement and the timing of the movement can be explored. Such a question as, "Are we making big movements or small movements?" emphasizes spatial relationships.

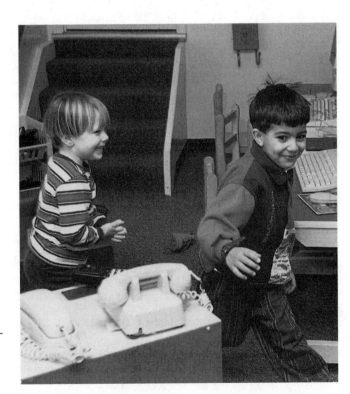

These boys have been encouraged to talk about the way in which they are traveling, thus they will be describing the movement they have chosen to do.

We can learn a great deal about each child's language development as we engage children in describing their actions. You may observe a child who cannot talk while moving, because it takes so much energy and concentration to do the movement. Remember that children's language development takes time, and that their own actions provide an excellent starting point to begin the process of describing movement.

Suggested Activities—Talking About Movement While Doing It

1. Large-group time or outside time are excellent occasions to encourage children to consciously explore various ways to move their arms or legs. Suggest movement activities that use various body positions (lying on one's back, stomach, or side; kneeling; sitting; standing): "What can our legs do when we are lying down on our backs? Let's all try some leg movements. David has thought of a way to move his legs. David, can you tell us how your legs are moving? Let's try David's way. Who has another way we can move our legs? Betsy, how are you moving? Let's all try what Betsy is doing. Can we do it slower? Can we do it faster?"

2. In the play yard or classroom suggest that the children find different ways to walk across a balance beam. (These suggestions might include walking with the body short or tall; walking forward, backward, sideways; walking quickly or slowly.) Ask each child to describe how he or she is performing the task. If a child doesn't respond, ask questions that will help that child describe the task: "Was your body short or tall?" You also can ask other children to watch and describe the child's movement.

3. During work time in the preschool, observe the way children are moving. Join them when appropriate—copying what they are doing. Encourage the children to describe their actions; repeat what they say and, when possible, expand on their statements so children will hear a more comprehensive description of their movements.

Planning Movement Before Doing It

It's outside time, and a group of children are playing on the slide. Warren, the adult, says to the child next in line, "James, tell us how you are going to go down the slide." Then, as Sally approaches, Warren asks, "Sally, can you slide down in another way? Can you tell us how you are going to do it?" It's Marwan's turn next, and Warren asks, "Marwan, can you find something to do with your arms while you slide down the slide? What will you do?"

In this scenario Warren is encouraging each child to plan the play activity before doing it and to use language to describe the plan. When children are asked to describe their plans for movement, it implies that they will give some thought to their actions before performing them. Thus movement takes on a new meaning. The adult is the *facilitator,* encouraging the child to choose how to perform a movement, while the child is *owner* of the movement and is accountable for making a plan and carrying it out. The description may be very primitive or very elaborate; the important thing is that it reflects a thoughtful decision—the key to purposeful movement.

Young children who learn to think through a movement *before* doing it will be better able to master the more advanced motor tasks that come with maturation: playing baseball, swimming, riding a bicycle.

Suggested Activities—Planning Movement Before Doing It

1. At large-group time encourage children to describe, before they move, how they are going to move around the outside of the group and back to their places. (This is to encourage thinking about different possible locomotor movements before the action takes place.) For a range of movements to help children explore, see "Moving in Locomotor Ways," page 80.

2. In a singing game such as "Someone Is the Leader" in *Movement Plus Rhymes, Songs, and Singing Games* (Weikart, 1997) ask a child to suggest a movement and to demonstrate it for the other children to follow. In doing this, the child may describe and then demonstrate, or may simultaneously demonstrate and describe the action. In either case, the child is achieving the goal of thinking about doing a movement and using language to describe the plan.

3. When preschool children are outside playing follow-the-leader, ask the next "leader" to describe what he or she is going to do before beginning.

4. During planning time in the preschool suggest that each of the children in your planning group think of a movement to go with their plan. Each child describes a plan and then demonstrates the accompanying movement. You may wish to repeat what the child says and then expand on the child's original statement, or you may ask relevant questions about the plan, thus getting the child to think more about it.

Steven has made a plan for how he will go down the hill on the sled. He now is executing his plan.

Recalling Movement After Completion

Samuel walks across the balance beam and then Phyllis, the adult, asks, "Samuel, can you remember how you went across the beam?" (Phyllis has already asked Samuel to plan his walk first and now is asking questions to help him recall more specifically how the task was accomplished. Questions to choose from might include the following: "What else can you tell us about how you traveled? What direction were you facing? How tall was your body when you went across the beam? Where did you put your arms to help you keep your balance? How quickly did you travel across the beam?") Then Phyllis demonstrates a simple movement and asks Samuel to describe it. (She could also ask him to do what she just did and then to recall it.) Phyllis is not concerned when Samuel finds it necessary to repeat the task while recalling it, because she understands that children's developmental levels vary and that this is the way Samuel is able to understand the movement.

⁂

Phyllis's role in this scenario is to help Samuel think back to a task that was just completed and to review what he just did. This helps her assess Samuel's level of kinesthetic awareness. The ability to recall a motor task, without repeat-

After Gerald completes his plan, he will be asked to recall the movements he is doing. Different children in these scenes have shared their plans for movement and have then recalled their actions.

ing it, is a fairly advanced task; even adults must sometimes resort to a reenactment of a movement in order to recall and describe it, particularly if they haven't thought about it before doing the movement.

Recall—a time for reviewing what was done during **work** time—is part of the daily routine (the plan-do-review sequence in the High/Scope Preschool Curriculum). This means that children are attuned to reflecting on what they have done, and recalling movement fits well with this manner of thinking.

Suggested Activities—Recalling Movement After Completion

1. Ask children to recall what they did with their bodies in a singing game such as "Jenny Mouse" from *Movement Plus Rhymes, Songs, & Singing Games* (Weikart, 1997). Many of the children will repeat their movements as they recall, and this type of repetition should be encouraged and supported.

2. Ask children what they did first and second in a two-task obstacle course. If you ask for a volunteer to describe the two tasks and then the child can't remember what was done, you could ask the child to repeat the obstacle course and then to review what occurred.

3. Ask the children to find a special way to come to the snack table. Ways children might choose include crawling, jumping, hopping, walking backward. After they arrive, ask them to describe how they came to the table. Some will not remember. Some will repeat what another child says. Some may not say anything. In these cases you can demonstrate how a specific child came to the table and then ask the target child to describe that movement.

Learner SAY & DO (Linking a Single Movement to a Single Word)

Preschool children at large-group time are chanting "knees, knees, knees, knees" while tapping their knees with both hands simultaneously. The children are learning to connect a movement with the word that names the part of the body involved. The children have established a common beat, created by the chant, that enables them to perform the movement together. The movement is maintained at a steady tempo with the addition of the words.

One way for young children to combine action, thought, and language effectively is to link a single movement to a single word. *The above scenario involves the SAY & DO method of linking actions to words.* All movement involves **timing.** If children have words to speak to create the tempo for a particular movement or sequence of movements, they then have a strategy for developing steady beat timing and coordination. More information about the SAY & DO method of identifying steady beat and supporting movement coordination is contained in Chapter 4 under "Feeling and Expressing Steady Beat" and "Moving in Sequences to a Common Beat."

"Chin, chin, chin, chin." The SAY & DO method of linking actions with words enables children to connect a movement with the word that names the body part involved.

Suggested Activities—Linking a Single Movement to a Single Word (SAY & DO)

1. Ask the children to tap their knees with both hands. After children have tried this, demonstrate for them the SAY & DO method—tap your knees and say "knees" each time your hands touch your knees. Then have the children try it. Some children may need hands-on guidance at first in order to link the movement with the word.

2. Ask the children to march around the room, or in a circle, to their own beat and to say the word "march" with each step. Then have them march all together, while chanting the word "march." Keep in mind that the SAY & DO method of linking locomotor movement with words is much more difficult to accomplish at the preschool level. Nonlocomotor movement with SAY & DO is easier.

3. Encourage children to explore how to bend and straighten their arms. Ask them to describe what their arms are doing. Then suggest several different ways of bending and straightening the arms, for example, to the side, in front, overhead with the body short, with the body tall. Encourage children to talk about what they are doing while moving, or plan how they will move before moving, or recall what they did upon completing the movement. After they have explored the movement in these ways, set up a common chant of "bend, straighten" or "out, in," and link the words and actions to enable the children to perform together and develop an even deeper level of understanding.

Summary of Describing Movement

Both of the movement key experiences *acting upon movement directions* and *describing movement* provide children with various ways to link action, thought, and language. Engaging in these processes helps children develop a deeper understanding of their movements. Adults can support children in these activities by becoming actively involved with children at their level of understanding and interest. With preschoolers, adults can pose problems and ask questions that help the children become even more aware of their developing body coordination abilities and their physical movements.

By following the suggestions presented in this chapter, you can help young children become more aware of the various parts of their body and how they move. We call this **kinesthetic awareness.** Besides *acting upon movement directions,* the children are also developing their language skills by using words to describe their movements (the *describing movement* key experience). To describe movement, children must have opportunities to **listen to language about movement** in order to use it themselves. Second, children must be encouraged to **talk about movement while doing it.** Further, they must be encouraged to **plan movement before doing it** and to **recall movement after completing it.** And finally, a useful way to further link action, thought, and language is to have children use the **learner SAY & DO** method.

These aspects of **engaging the learner** through *acting upon movement activities* and *describing movement* will take on more significance in the next chapter, which explains the process of **enabling the learner.**

Enabling the Learner— Ways to Move 3

Adults can prepare children for lifelong learning and enjoyment of movement-related concepts and activities by initiating and supporting their development in three broad areas of movement exploration. These three areas correspond to the three key experiences in the **enabling the learner** category: *moving in nonlocomotor ways, moving in locomotor ways,* and *moving with objects.* Once children have enough experience in these movement areas, they will be much more aware of the body, language, space, and time concepts related to each.

This chapter focuses on ways to enable children to move comfortably. It answers such questions as the following: How can we help children develop the language awareness, the coordination, the balance, the patterns of movement, and the comfort with movement that they will need to be successful with many more complicated movement sequences when they are older? How can we provide opportunities that permit children to explore the use of their bodies in personal space? How can we encourage and guide them to make their own movement discoveries?

The three key experiences discussed in the three major sections of this chapter will provide adults with many enjoyable movement activities that are suitable for young children. Before we begin these discussions, however, some definition of terms is in order. What exactly do we mean when we say "nonlocomotor movement," "locomotor movement," and "movement with objects"?

These children are using personal space for nonlocomotor movement and locomotor movement. In two of the photos, the rings identify each child's personal space.

- **Nonlocomotor movement**—This is movement that always has one part of the body anchored to the floor. It is performed in one's own space (personal space) without completely transferring body weight. For example, moving some part of the upper body or of the lower body when seated or lying down is nonlocomotor. Moving only one side of the lower body while standing, and rocking from side to side while both feet remain on the floor, are other examples.

- **Locomotor movement**—This is movement that does not have a body part anchored to the floor. It can be performed in personal space (marching in place, hopping, jumping) or it can involve moving around the wider, available area (general space), with the body not anchored and with complete transfers of weight. Examples (involving just the lower body) are walking, jumping, galloping, skipping. (Lower-body locomotor movement, which involves complete transfers of weight and therefore foot patterns, will be stressed in this book.) Examples (involving upper and/or lower body) are rolling, crawling, climbing, walking on the hands.

- **Movement with objects**—This type of movement occurs when either of the two types of movement just described (nonlocomotor or locomotor) is performed *in a pur-*

In these pictures children are exploring locomotor movement by discovering different ways to jump, including jumping off objects.

poseful way with one or more objects. The object might be a ball, bat, racquet, rhythm instrument, jump-rope, beanbag, paper plate, paintbrush, scissors, or pencil, to name a few. The object might also be some kind of outdoor play equipment, but issues related to using such specialized kinds of objects and equipment are left to other books.

Even though the key experiences involving nonlocomotor movement, locomotor movement, and movement with objects are presented in separate sections, the intent is to have children work with these experiences interchangeably *rather than master each one in sequence*. Although there is a broad range of activity choices among these three key experiences, it is important that adults consider the level of difficulty of the movement in relation to the children's present competencies. It is equally important that adults know how to initiate a movement so the child can achieve success or so that the

The children are showing how they balance on one foot. The adults know how important it is to have these children try to balance on the other foot as well.

child will want to work with it enough to achieve success. Young children should not be expected to master a new movement without a great deal of experience. The most effective time to work with new movement usually occurs when children are playing alone or with peers. It is this "informal practice" that is missed when children have few opportunities for "natural play" experiences. When adults are present, they should participate with the children and talk with them about the movement in which they all are engaged, rather than pass judgment or correct a movement that the children are exploring.

To help adults work successfully with children in these major areas of movement learning, I have devised a set of "Comfort With Movement" teaching guidelines. These guidelines should be kept in mind when introducing all three types of movement; they are summarized in Chart 3.1 and are discussed next.

Guidelines for Using the "Comfort With Movement" Teaching Progression

1. **Devise ways for students to be as inconspicuous as possible.** Avoid calling on a child to be the leader for movement until you are certain the child will be able to respond. Also, a child who seems to sit back a bit at large-group time probably needs time to watch the activities before joining in.

2. **Initiate movement without reference to specific sides of the body (right or left).** If a particular movement involves using or beginning with only one side of the body, refer to it as "one side" or the "favorite side" or "either side." Then be sure to encourage children to also try the movement with the "other side." Assure children that alternating movements can begin on either side.

3. **Try to avoid posing movement problems that have a definite "right" and "wrong" solution.** Children's initial explorations should involve doing a movement in the way they choose to do it. Give them lots of opportunities to explore the movement in their own way and eventually they will understand how to do it.

Chart 3.1

*Comfort With Movement
Teaching Guidelines—A Summary*

1. Devise ways for children to be as inconspicuous as possible.
2. Initiate movement without reference to specific sides of the body (right or left).
3. Try to avoid setting up situations that have a "right" and "wrong" solution.
4. Introduce locomotor movement in personal space before general space.
5. Use movement and creative representation experiences that are age-appropriate.
6. Introduce action songs and other movements for rhymes or songs by presenting the movement first.

---

4. **Introduce locomotor movement experiences in personal space before general space.** Many locomotor movements such as marching, jumping, and hopping can be performed in personal space before they are done in general space. This strategy gives students a chance to develop the balance and coordination the movement requires.

5. **Use movement and creative representation experiences that are age-appropriate.** Patting parts of the body such as the head, chin, or ears is appropriate for young children. Also, young children delight in moving in ways that represent events or animals. After a trip to the zoo, for example, children often want to move about as if they were the monkey or tiger they just saw. Encourage children to do this and to talk about their movement and why they thought the animal moved that way.

6. **Introduce action songs and other movements for rhymes or songs by presenting the movement first.** When children are successful with the movement, layer on the rhyme or song. John, an adult in the preschool, wanted to introduce a new action song "Start Your Day With a Hug" from *Movement Plus Rhymes, Songs, & Singing Games* (Weikart, 1997). First, John demonstrated the actions one at a time and encouraged the children to join him. Then he had them describe each action and recall the order of them. Finally, John sang the song, pausing to give children time to respond with one of the actions.

Key Experience:
Moving in Nonlocomotor Ways

In this section, we explore nonlocomotor movement in depth. To amplify the definition just given, "nonlocomotor" refers to movement with any part or parts of the body that is performed in one's personal space. It is movement that does not result in a transfer of weight, as does walking in place, jumping, or hopping. It can be movement of the arms, head, trunk, hips, or legs. (It can be movement of both legs in a seated or lying down position, or movement of one leg while a person is standing in a balanced position.) Nonlocomotor movement can also be movement of fingers and toes, hands and feet, or shoulders. Nonlocomotor movement can be executed with both large (gross-motor) and small (fine-motor) movements, but we will concern ourselves here only with gross-motor movement. Fine-motor movements are more appropriate for the school-aged child; preschoolers are more comfortable with and more able to engage in gross-motor movements.

Nonlocomotor movement is the easiest form of movement because it is performed in a seated, prone, or kneeling position, or in a standing position without weight transfer. As you watch a group of children at play, you will observe that they are performing numerous nonlocomotor movements, often in combination with locomotor movements. You will see that some children swing their arms; others twist their bodies; others stretch or, in sequence, bend and then straighten their arms and legs.

Young children love to explore various positions for nonlocomotor movement.

Now let's look more closely at nonlocomotor movement. Nonlocomotor *arm patterns* are used in pointing, tossing, or throwing a ball; in swinging a plastic bat, stick, or flag; or when moving creatively to music. Nonlocomotor *leg patterns* are used when bouncing, when swinging a leg side to side, when kicking or trapping a ball, or when pumping the legs while swinging. The arm movements that are part of a singing game or action song are all based on nonlocomotor experiences. If children have not had enough opportunities to perform nonlocomotor movement in these general ways, they may find it difficult to master the specific movements needed for a particular song or game.

Four prerequisites seem to be needed for children to be successful with these types of movement experiences:

- **Language competence.** Children will need to learn the names of the parts of the body that will be used for movement. The child will use his or her emerging language skills either to understand or to generate the words that describe or label a particular type of movement. The child will also use language to understand or generate the words describing the quality of a movement (such as *smooth, quick, bumpy).* The child will use language to understand and identify spatial relationships (such as *high, low, in front of, in back of).* The child will use language to identify concepts of space and time, for example, the direction of a movement *(up, down)* and the tempo of a movement *(fast, slow).* (The section in Chapter 2 that can help children in this regard is "Describing Movement."

- **Balance.** The ability to maintain equilibrium is essential. If a child's sense of balance is "off," his or her performance will be affected adversely. Numerous experiences with play activities that require balance usually strengthen and expand a child's ability in this area.

- **Minimal level of coordination.** As with experiences achieving balance, if children are given numerous opportunities to play, the basic foundations for coordination usually are developed in natural ways. In addition, achieving steady beat competence—that is accurately feeling and expressing beat (see Chapter 4)—seems to aid children in developing coordination.

These children are exploring different ways to swing their arms.

- **Strength.** Young children must have sufficient play opportunities that involve using and strengthening their large muscles. If children do not run and climb enough, they may lack the strength needed to perform the nonlocomotor movements presented here and the locomotor movements that follow.

Next we will examine the **essential elements of nonlocomotor movement:**

1. Recognizing the various body positions used to explore nonlocomotor movement

2. Developing body awareness with specific attention to the types of movement that can be performed by parts of the body

3. Developing language awareness

4. Developing space awareness, including awareness of space and of movement variations

5. Developing time awareness.

Body Positions for Nonlocomotor Movement

It's large-group time in the preschool. The children are exploring with Maria, their teacher, how to move their legs while they are seated—movements they probably have done without thought many times. They discover that they can only move their legs in front of their bodies while seated and that they can't lift their legs very high and still maintain their balance. Maria asks, "How can we make our legs go in back of us?" The children try different things and, eventually, with Maria's guidance, realize that they have to change their body position to accomplish the task.

This scenario illustrates that children are not apt to realize the limitations that body position places on movement, or the freedom of movement allowed by some body positions, unless they are given opportunities to engage in problem-solving movement activities in a variety of positions. The body positions that may be used in exploring nonlocomotor movement are as follows:

- Lying on one's back (supine position)

- Lying on one's stomach (prone position)

- Lying on one's side (side position)

- Sitting down with legs straight in front, or in a "V" shape in front of the body, or folded close to the body

- Kneeling on hands and knees, just on the knees, or curled in a ball

- Standing with feet close together or with feet apart

We need to help children explore movement from these different perspectives, remembering to support and encourage their discoveries, as discussed in the previous chapter.

As long as a child's body remains anchored in some way, the body can assume various shapes and statue games can be played. Encourage children to be creative and to try nonlocomotor movement from a number of positions. You will be amazed at the inventiveness and creativity they will show!

Suggested Activities—Body Positions for Nonlocomotor Movement

1. Have the children copy you in a lying down (on your side) position. Once they are in this position, suggest some movements they might try—for example, "Touch your hand to your knee. Pat your knee slowly." Ask for volunteers to choose other movements the group might try. Then have the children find another position and ask "How are you lying on the floor now?" Encourage them to suggest movements and ask the other children to find out if they can do the movement from their position.

2. Encourage the children to choose any position they wish and say to them "What parts of the body are touching the floor?" Pose questions like these: "Is your head touching the floor? Are your hands touching the floor? What else is touching the floor?" Encourage all children to respond naturally or call on individual children who seem ready to respond.

3. Pose a movement problem for the children: "How many positions can you put your body in while both your feet and both hands touch the floor?" Encourage the children to talk about the positions as they move. As in the other activities, if chil-

These two children are being rocked by Phyllis and Ruth, the adults in the classroom, as a third child watches. They're learning that their body position does limit their movement possibilities!

dren want to demonstrate their positions to other children, encourage them to do so and suggest that the other children try to copy the positions and talk about the movements.

Developing Body Awareness Through Nonlocomotor Movement

During outside time children are exploring different ways to swing their arms. Charles, the adult, asks, "How can we swing our arms? Jill is swinging her arms in front of her. Let's all follow Jill and swing both arms in front of our bodies. How does the swing outside move? Can we make our arms move the way the swing moves? What did we do?"

Children have achieved body awareness when they understand how each part of the body can move and what movement relationships exist among body parts. Experiences involving nonlocomotor movement are an ideal opportunity for developing this awareness. Of course, body awareness must be based on knowing the locations of different parts of the body—knowledge that most children begin to develop before kindergarten age. Games of body awareness can be played in the home or with caregivers beginning when children reach the age of 2.

There are **12 basic nonlocomotor movements**—ones that young children can do while remaining in personal space with their bodies anchored or fixed in some way:

bend	**straighten**	**curl**	**stretch**
twist	**turn**	**push**	**pull**
swing	**rock**	**rise**	**fall**

Bend. Think about what areas of the body can bend. The neck can bend sideward and also forward and backward. (Because of the stress it puts on the spine, bending the neck should not be encouraged.) The arms, together or separately, can bend at the elbows, and the hands can bend at the wrist. Legs can bend at the knees. The entire body can bend at the waist, going forward, backward, or sideward. As with bending the head, bending the body backward at the waist should be done only with care.

Straighten. Straightening is usually thought of in connection with bending, which creates a sequence of movements. For example, the arms might bend at the elbows and then straighten. The body might bend forward at the waist and then return to a straight position. While lying down or standing, one can bend both knees and then straighten them. Straightening can also include straightening one's back (sitting up straight) from a slouched position.

Twist. Various parts of the body—arms, legs, waist, neck—can twist, which means to rotate partially. At the shoulder (or hip) arms (or legs) can twist, thus rotating part of the way around before returning to twist in the other direction.

Twisting implies a partial rotation. If the elbow is bent, the forearm can twist without the entire arm twisting. The same is true of the lower leg when the leg is bent at the knee. The neck and trunk can twist partially around.

Turn. Turning takes the arm, hand, finger, foot, or leg all the way around in a 360-degree movement. The movement, which involves the body part tracing a circle as it fully rotates around a single point (such as the arm tracing a circle in the air as it rotates from the shoulder) is a turning motion rather than a twist. The hand, of course, rotates at the wrist; the finger, at the knuckle; the foot, at the ankle; and the leg, at the hip. The head might also turn around to describe a circle, but this is not advisable because of the force it exerts on the neck. Likewise, turning the upper body fully around at the waist is possible, but this may exert undue force on the spine. Young children are sometimes observed turning one arm quickly around in a "windup" motion.

Swing. We use this term for a two-way motion, like that of a child's swing. For example, the two-way swing of a leg might be forward and backward, or sideward, from one side to the other. Swinging may mean two arms or two legs moving together, one arm or leg moving by itself, or the two arms or two legs moving in an alternating pattern (one arm swinging forward as the other swings

These children in the block area are physically active, yet they are also moving in many nonlocomotor ways. They are using their space awareness skills to accomplish their tasks, and the girl at right is balancing on two wooden blocks as she "directs traffic"!

backward). The arms and legs swing from the shoulder and hip joint, respectively. Obviously, to swing both legs, a person would have to be in a position that removes weight from the legs (e.g., lying down).

Rock. This is sometimes referred to as "swaying." Rocking implies a partial shift, but not a full transfer, of weight. Rocking can be sideward (from one side to the other), or forward and backward. If a child is sitting and rocking, the body weight shifts almost enough to cause loss of balance, but the body rocks back before balance is lost. When a child is standing and rocking, both feet remain on the floor as the body weight shifts from side to side or forward and backward; rocking forward and backward in this case means rocking with one foot forward and the other backward. *Note:* When rocking sideward, if the child's foot leaves the floor as he or she rocks to the side, a complete transfer of weight occurs in place, and therefore the rocking becomes locomotor (not anchored) movement, as steps are taken first on one side and then the other side.

Push. This is a movement away from the body that implies a steady force being applied to the body part that is performing it. It might be thought of as simulating a pushing action against an object. Pushing may be done with the arms or legs and involves the concept of intensity (to be discussed later). Regardless of which limb is involved in pushing, it is safer for that limb to remain partially bent rather than fully extended.

Pull. This is the opposite movement from pushing and applies steady force toward the body. We usually think of pulling with the arms, because the movement usually involves grasping an object. It is, however, also possible to simulate grasping and pulling an object with the arms or legs.

Curl. Three parts of the body can curl: fingers, toes, and the spine. These are

At this large-group time, the children are following their teacher, Phyllis, who is initiating bending and straightening the legs.

the only body parts that curl, because curling can only occur at joints where there are short bones on each side of a joint. A joint with long bones on each side (such as an elbow or knee) is not suitable for a curling motion, so legs and arms are not able to curl.

Stretch. This movement is often paired with curling, as bending was paired with straightening by describing the two movements as opposites. Actually, it is possible to stretch from a straight position to a hyper-extended (straighter) position of the arms, legs, or spine without first bending or curling. Stretching upon awakening in the morning, for example, is hyper-extension of the arms, legs, and spine. Stretching is usually a fluid motion, with the stretch being long, gradual, and accompanied by force—rather than short in duration.

Rise. Just as the whole body can move forward, backward, sideward, and around, so can it move upward and downward. If the entire body moves in an upward direction, this is rising. We rise, for example, from a squat or low position.

Fall. This movement is the opposite of rising. It consists of allowing the body to move in a downward direction, often to a squat position or falling all the way down.

In addition to these 12 basic nonlocomotor movements, there are innumerable other gross-motor and fine-motor nonlocomotor actions that children can explore. Some examples of these actions are listed here:

touch	**thump**	**pound**
punch	**dab**	**slash**
shake	**wring**	**flick**
clap	**snap**	**float**

Narrowly demonstrating or describing many of these actions for children is not only difficult but also inadvisable. It is better to allow room for children to bring something of their own interpretation to a nonlocomotor action. One child's way of shaking may be different from another child's way of shaking, for example. An adult might say (before demonstrating), "This is one way to shake. Can you think of other ways to shake?" As children explore movement of the arms, fingers, legs, and feet, encourage them to use their own words to describe their actions. They will thus be combining these actions with language awareness, which is discussed in the next section. Children often have special words for their actions.

 ## Suggested Activities—Developing Body Awareness Through Nonlocomotor Movement

1. Bend and straighten both arms and ask the children to do it with you. Then ask the children to talk about what they are doing. The goal for the children is to have them use many words to describe the bending and

straightening movement, words such as "out/in" or "open/close" or "push/pull" or "far/near." Tell the children that other words for the movement are "bend" and "straighten," and then ask the children "Can you find a way to bend and straighten your arms that is different from the way we just tried? Can you find other parts of the body that you can bend and straighten? Let's try it! Who wants to be the leader to show us a way to bend and straighten?"

2. Help the children explore the words "curl" and "stretch": "Does anyone have a kitten at home? How does the kitten curl up in your lap? Let's pretend we are kittens and curl our bodies. Can we curl just our fingers? Just our toes? How does the kitten stretch when it wakes up? How do you stretch in the morning? Can you find another way to stretch? Can we stretch our fingers, our toes, our whole body? Can we stretch while we are sitting? Is there another way we can stretch?"

3. Suggest that children explore some swinging movements, first with both arms, then with one arm and then the other arm. After they have done a number of these swinging movements, ask the children if they can swing other parts of the body. Ask individual children to volunteer to be the leader and show a swinging movement that the other children can copy. Ask each child, before showing the movement, to describe how he or she is going to move, thereby requiring planning.

Developing Language Awareness Through Nonlocomotor Movement

The preschoolers have been working with action words from the story Beth, their teacher, is reading. Each time Beth comes to an action word in the story, she suggests that the children choose a movement to explore the word's meaning.

The children are learning that language provides the labels for nonlocomotor movement. Words come to life when their meaning is explored through movement. As the children are twisting their arms, for example, Beth encourages them to give their movements various labels, such as "out/in," or "over/under." At some point, she can refer to the movement as "twisting."

How can we make sure children have opportunities to hear and eventually use the words that describe movement? As was pointed out in discussing the key experience *describing movement* in Chapter 2, we can use a movement vocabulary with children from a very early age. As we comment on specific movements that we or the children make, we are helping them achieve cognitive understanding of purposeful movement. As children attach meaning to words by exploring purposeful movement, they will begin to understand the language of nonlocomotor movement. As children listen to language about movement, as they talk about the movement they are doing, as they use language to plan and to recall their movements, they are developing language awareness. They are on the road to literacy.

Suggested Activities—Developing Language Awareness Through Nonlocomotor Movement

1. At large-group time in your preschool, suggest that the children sing "Hokey Pokey." (See the variation in *Movement Plus Rhymes, Songs, & Singing Games* Weikart, 1997.) The two nonlocomotor movements used in this singing game are instigated with the words "put your two hands up and put your two hands down." These two movements are followed by another locomotor movement "turn both arms around." Before making your suggestion, indicate to the children that you are going to introduce a singing game and that you will use the movement words "put up," "put down," and "turn around." Once underway, suggest that the children might want to use different body parts to "put up" and "put down"—then suggest that the children imitate the movements they see others doing. Encourage them to talk about each movement.

2. Each day, explore with your preschoolers the meaning of a different movement word. For example, explore the word "turn." During movement time have the children identify different parts of the body they can turn and different ways to turn them. Begin with this question: "Can our arms turn? Let's see how many ways we can turn our arms." After the children try out various movements in this way, ask a volunteer to demonstrate his or her movement.

3. At recall time in your preschool, encourage the children to talk about their activities and to demonstrate movement. For example, one adult asked these questions: "Sherry, can you tell us how you cut with the scissors?" "Alan, can you tell us how you pounded the nail with the hammer? How you sawed the wood?" "Who else wants to talk about something they did at work time?" "Sally, what did you pretend to do?" In this way, the children use language to recall and demonstrate their experiences using nonlocomotor movement.

Developing Space Awareness Through Nonlocomotor Movement

Some children are playing in the block area during work time. They are building towers of different sizes and they are laying roadways for their cars. All the while, they are physically active and are involved in interesting movement activities. In addition, as they talk with one another, they are using language to describe various spatial concepts and movements. Rosie and Sue, the adults in the preschool, begin to introduce other spatial con-

cepts and to ask open-ended questions such as "Josie, you're piling the blocks on top of each other—is there some other way you could arrange them?"

Children's space awareness has to do with realizing their movement's relationship to their own bodies in personal space. This means understanding the "where" and "how" of nonlocomotor movement. The "where" of nonlocomotor movement involves the following concepts:

in(side)/out(side)	**in front of/in back of**
around/through	**near/far**
up/down	**between/alongside**
on/off	**over/under**

These "where" concepts give added meaning to the movements the children perform. For example, a child may be made aware of shaking both hands *in front of* or *in back of* the body or of bending and straightening the arms *up* and *down*.

The "how" of nonlocomotor movement for young children involves these concepts:

direction	**size**
level	**intensity (force)**
pathway	**timing**

Each of these concepts is explained here in terms of nonlocomotor movement. In connection with *moving in locomotor ways,* the next key experience, we will have more to say about these spatial relationships and extension concepts.

Direction. Does the nonlocomotor movement (the bending, pushing, stretching, and so on) go upward and downward? Does the movement go forward and then backward (as a swinging movement might)? Does it go sideward or back and forth (as a rocking movement might)? Does the movement go partially around (as a twisting movement would) or all the way around (as a turning movement would)? Does the movement go over or under another part of the body? Does the movement go out (as a push away from the body) and in (as a pull toward the body)? These are the directional concepts that can be explored with young children in simple and gradually more sophisticated ways, depending on their age and experience. All movement has a directional aspect.

Level. The level of a movement indicates whether it is performed in a high, middle, or low plane. Below the knees, as one is standing, is usually thought of as low level; anywhere between the knees and shoulders is middle level; and anywhere above that is high level. (With preschool children we generally omit the middle level.) You might ask children if they are swinging their arms high— or low. Or, as a movement problem to solve, ask them how they might bend and straighten their legs at a high level. Later, when objects are added to movement, it is meaningful to ask such questions as, "Did you catch the ball up high? Or down low?" "At what level do you want to wave your scarf?"

Size. A nonlocomotor movement's size may be large, medium, or small (big and little terms are often used with younger children). For example, an arm might turn to make a little or a big circle. A swing of the leg might be a big swing—or a little swing. (Increasing the size of a movement often increases its intensity, which is an extension concept.)

Pathway. Just as a pencil draws various kinds of lines on paper, you can think of a moving body (or body part) as drawing straight, curved, or zigzag pathways on the ground or in the air. For example, when swinging arms forward and backward, you can think of the finger tips as describing a

Climbing on one of the unique structures on the High/Scope playground, Yvette is developing strength as well as balance and coordination.

curved pathway in the air. Moving one hand from left to right in front of the body to denote a musical phrase describes a straight (or perhaps a curved) pathway. As both legs bend and straighten (starting low and moving higher and higher) while one is lying on the back, the feet describe a zigzag pathway.

Intensity. This refers to the force of a nonlocomotor movement—whether it is strong or weak. For example, pushing or pulling can be strong or weak. Bending and straightening can also be performed with little or great force, as can twisting, turning, etc.

Timing. Nonlocomotor movement is affected by another extension—the **timing** of the movement. Timing—**time awareness**—is described in the next section.

Suggested Activities—Developing Space Awareness Through Nonlocomotor Movement

1. Select contrasting elements, such as *up/down,* and guide the children through an exploration of this direction. After performing an up or down movement, say to the children "I made my arms go up. Can you make your arms go up? Can we find another way to make them go up?" For children who are familiar with "Eensy, Beensy Spider," ask how the spider goes up the water spout. "How does the rain come down? Let's make the rain come down in another way. Is there any other part of the body we can make go up and then come down? Look, Jimmy is making his whole body go up and down. Let's all of us do that." Encourage differ-

ent children to show how they are doing the movements and to tell the rest of the class about them. During outside time encourage the children to go *up* the ladder and *down* the slide. Use these words throughout the day.

2. Work with the children on understanding the spatial concepts of *in front of/in back of* by giving a few simple verbal directions: "Put your arms in front of you. Put them in back of you. Put them in front of you on the floor. In back of you on the floor. In front of your face. In back of your head. Can you put your legs in front of you? In back of you? Can you put your legs in front of you and your arms in back of you?" Encourage children to use the terms, also: "Where are my elbows?" (in front) "Where are they now?" (in back) "Let's see you put your elbows in front. In back. Who can tell us some part of the body we can put in front of us or in back of us?"

3. Encourage children to explore the basic nonlocomotor movement of *twisting,* during which they will be using a number of spatial relationships. For example, say "Let's find a way to twist our arms. Where are you twisting your arms? Can you find a new place to twist your arms? Can any other parts of the body twist? Can we twist our arms and bend and straighten our legs too? That's hard, isn't it? Can we make our arms go up and down while we are twisting them?"

Developing Time Awareness Through Nonlocomotor Movement

Children are in the play yard. Cynthia, an adult in the child care setting, sees that there are tremendous variations in the pacing of their movements. Some seem to move at a rapid pace, while others are very slow and deliberate in their movements. Some children start and stop a lot during their play.

All movement varies in time, just as all movement varies in use of the body and use of space. The **time awareness concepts** that can be developed with young children as they perform nonlocomotor movements are these:

start/stop   **fast/slow**   **getting faster/getting slower**

Clearly the "where" and "how" of nonlocomotor movement are closely interrelated with the time awareness concepts. For example, a shaking movement can be done *in front of* the body, and *down low* (the "where" and "how" of the movement direction or level), and *fast* (the time awareness of the movement).

Singing games, movements to music, and action songs use nonlocomotor movement. Because these activities are performed in specific timing, have the children work with the movements before the song or game is added. For example, you can introduce the "Ring Around the Rosey" melody by singing to the children "Turn your arms *slowly*" (three times) and then "Turn them *fast*" on the "All fall down."

Suggested Activities—Developing Time Awareness Through Nonlocomotor Movement

1. Spread chairs around the activity space, providing one chair for each child. Ask the children to be seated. Say "When you hear the music start, move all of your body. When the music stops, you stop." Start the music so the children begin to move. After a short time, stop the music so the children will stop moving. Each time the activity is repeated, a different child can start and stop the music or be the leader for all to follow.

2. With the children spaced comfortably apart in the activity space, ask "Can you move your arms very slowly? Can you move your arms quickly? Where are you moving your arms?" (Most children will first move their arms in front of their bodies.) "Find somewhere else to move your arms slowly. Now move them quickly." Children should explore movement over the head, behind their backs, down low, and so on. Have the children suggest the movement and whether they should be *slow* or *fast*.

3. Suggest that the children lie on their backs on the floor. Say "Find a movement you can do slowly with one leg. What movement did you choose? Can you do it with the other leg? Do it slowly with both legs? Do it quickly?" Continue the activity until several ways of moving have been explored, such as bending and straightening and twisting and turning. Have the children suggest leg movements that can be performed while lying on their backs in a slow or fast way.

Summary of Moving in Nonlocomotor Ways

Of course, for children, the key experience *moving in nonlocomotor ways* does not occur in isolation. All the concepts related to nonlocomotor movement that have been discussed here—the **body awareness, language awareness, space awareness,** and **time awareness concepts**—have relevance to the other key experiences. Aspects of nonlocomotor movement—including the **anchored positions, the 12 basic movements,** and **various other action words** —come into play when children are *acting upon movement directions* and *describing movement*. The goal for young children involved in nonlocomotor movement is to become knowledgeable about what their bodies can do in movement and to become comfortable with those movements.

To develop time awareness, Jennifer has suggested that the children move one of their arms very slowly over their head.

Next in this chapter, we look at another broad area of movement, which means another key experience important to **enabling the learner:** *moving in locomotor ways.*

Key Experience:
Moving in Locomotor Ways

If achieving comfort and ease with nonlocomotor movement is enabling for children, achieving the same results with locomotor movement is even more so. From watching helpless infants grow to relatively capable toddlers, we know that motor development begins with nonlocomotor (anchored body) movement and progresses to locomotor (nonanchored body) movement.

Locomotor movement like rolling, crawling, and walking, in which body weight is transferred and general space is used, presents new challenges to young children in terms of strength, balance, coordination, and timing. It is one thing to move smoothly, stop, start, avoid falling, avoid collisions, or go faster or slower while remaining anchored and in one's personal space. It is quite another to do all this while transferring weight in personal space or moving around an entire room or play space.

Phyllis, the adult, observes Evan as he hops across the block roadway he has constructed. Phyllis notes that Evan is going from one foot to the same foot in order to hop.

Locomotor movement in which the body remains upright, which is the focus of this discussion, can include everything from the first faltering walking steps that a child takes to the more mature movements of marching, jumping, hopping, and skipping. All of the variations of *moving in locomotor ways* with the body upright involve **foot patterns**—a complication that nonlocomotor movement does not present. Therefore, this discussion of how children develop comfort with locomotor movement, which again addresses **body, language, space,** and **time awareness,** will include an analysis of foot patterns involved in weight transfers.

As with the other movement key experiences, young children should be encouraged to explore these skills throughout the year. Although we cannot replicate their "natural play" experiences, we can approximate them as we provide opportunities for children and positive feedback on their efforts.

When we ask young children to move, they generally will choose to engage first in locomotor movement. To the young child, "moving" often implies traveling through space. Locomotor movement is movement through space, movement from one place to another, movement that projects the body in any direction in space. It involves transfers of weight. We generally list the basic locomotor movements as *walking, running, jumping,* and *hopping.* Extensions and variations of weight transfer result in *galloping, sliding,* and *skipping.* Because locomotor movement involves use of the lower extremities, young children without much experience moving in this way may appear very awkward at first. They lack the balance, coordination, and strength necessary to fully experience these free-flowing movements. Also, they may not know how to name (or label) the movements. For these reasons, there are several prerequisites to consider when selecting locomotor activities for young children.

- **The first prerequisite is *language competence.*** Does the child understand your request? For example, the child may be aware of the meaning of the words "walk" and "run," but may not understand the difference between "jumping" and "hopping."

- **The second prerequisite is *balance.*** Do the children have the balance necessary to do the task you wish to suggest, or do they seem to lose their balance easily? Can they move about without bumping into people, and can they stop without falling down?

- **The third prerequisite is a *minimal level of coordination.*** It takes coordination of the entire body to do locomotor movements. Children who lack basic body coordination cannot be expected to perform certain locomotor tasks, such as hopping or skipping; in fact, they may appear awkward when just walking.

- **The fourth prerequisite is *strength.*** Until children have developed sufficient strength, they cannot be expected to jump or hop. Children who walk early, or live in homes with no stairs or trees nearby to climb, or whose parents may not be aware of the importance of these early locomotor skills may need more experience in these areas. In these circumstances, we should offer the children enough experiences so that they will *gradually* become more proficient in movement skills. Crawling and climbing and rolling are critical early motor skills for young children. In these situations, opportunities should occur in a safe environment, free of "rights" and "wrongs," so young children will become comfortable with these patterns of movement. Adults should *engage* and *encourage* children rather than *direct* them.

As noted earlier, one of the results of the key experience *moving in locomotor ways* is for children to develop **body awareness, language awareness, space awareness,** and **time awareness.** Each type of awareness—as it applies to moving upright in general space, with transfers of weight—is explained next.

These children are using locomotor movement to travel around the large-group-time circle in their own ways! Occasionally, as in the photo below, it helps to have some children moving in personal space while others move about in general space.

Developing Body and Language Awareness in Locomotor Movement

It is outside time. Preschoolers are exploring different ways to move through space. Some are walking, some are running, some are galloping. Eva, an adult, says, "Watch me." After beginning her slides sidewards, Eva asks, "Can you do what I'm doing? I'm sliding." She is encouraging the children to try sliding. As the children try to slide, Eva asks, "What direction are you traveling? It seems as if you're traveling sidewards, too." Eva then encourages the children to explore sliding in the other direction around the yard, sliding with big and little steps, and sliding with the body up high and down low.

When working with young children on the various aspects of locomotor movement, **body awareness** involves helping them realize how their body weight is transferred—in other words, realizing what foot patterns are used.

When we think of only the locomotor movements that involve upright movement, these four are considered the **basic locomotor movements:**

walk	**run**
jump	**hop**

If those four movements are extended, combined, or varied, **four more basic movements** result:

leap	**gallop**
slide (gallop sideward)	**skip**

According to the type of weight transfer involved, each of the eight basic locomotor movements can be categorized as at least one of these:

1. Movement that transfers weight from one foot to the other foot in an even- or uneven-timing pattern. (Walking and running are even-timing examples of this category; galloping and sliding are uneven-timing examples of this category.)

2. Movement that transfers weight from two feet to two feet (jumping).

3. Movement that transfers weight from one foot to two feet (jumping).

4. Movement that transfers weight from two feet to one foot (leaping and hopping).

5. Movement that transfers weight from one foot to the same foot (hopping).

Leaping is a refinement of running that usually is considered appropriate for older children. Therefore, leaping will not be considered further in this section. However, if you should see a child leaping, use the occasion to engage the child in conversation about it.

Only one of the basic locomotor movements combines two of these categories. Skipping is a combination of Category 1 (a step) and Category 5 (a one-foot hop). Fuller explanations of the basic locomotor movements are presented next.

Walk. This is a *dynamic flow* of movement from one foot to the other. Considerable strength and balance are required for the child, at about age 1, to begin this transfer of weight. The body is in continuous contact with the walking surface throughout transferring weight from foot to foot.

Run. Like walking, this is a *dynamic flow* of movement from one foot to the other foot; it is usually a faster movement, however. Running should develop naturally at about age 2, starting as an exaggerated awkward-looking movement and developing into a movement with a smooth transition from one foot to the other. Running requires more strength and balance than walking, because both feet are off the floor between contacts of the forward leg with the running surface.

Jump. Jumping consists of a takeoff from two feet (or one foot) and a *landing on two feet*. A jump may send the body vertically upward, which would be jumping in personal space, or it may send the body forward for a distance, in general space.

Hop. This consists of taking off from one foot and then landing on the same foot. Compared to jumping, hopping requires more strength, balance, coordination, and basic timing because of the one-foot takeoff and *same-foot landing*. It is important to encourage children to hop on one foot and then on the other foot.

Gallop. Galloping is an uneven transfer of weight from one foot to the other foot. It occurs when one foot leads forward to take the weight as the rear foot quickly comes up to meet it, replacing the leading foot. The leading foot continues to lead throughout the gallop. Encourage children to lead with the other foot also. Adults can identify the timing by saying "BA-ba, BA-ba, BA-ba, BA-ba" as the children gallop.

Slide. This movement, like galloping, is an uneven transfer of weight from one foot to the other foot. The major difference is that the slide is performed sideward, whereas the gallop is usually done in a forward direction. Thus, the slide may be thought of as a sideward gallop. It is important that the children learn to slide in both directions. The timing is the same as the gallop.

Skip. As noted earlier, skipping is a combination of two *different* categories of weight transfer—one foot to the other foot, and one foot to the same foot— a step and then a hop. The timing is uneven, as in the gallop and slide. The first transfer of weight, the step, is the longer part of the skip, with the hop being the shorter. Skipping is the most difficult of the fundamental locomotor movement skills because the nonpreferred side must copy the same two movements (step, hop) that the preferred side has just done. Many children do not learn to hop on the nonpreferred side and instead do what I call a "half-skip." Children should be able to skip by the time they enter kindergarten.

Of course, learning to execute these locomotor movements involves learning the language of locomotor movement as well. **Language awareness** means not only that children understand the term *locomotor movement* and the words (labels) used for specific locomotor movements but also that they use those words to plan and identify what they are doing. Along with learning to label the basic movements (listed here), children can gradually become familiar with the words that extend these movements and then use those words to plan and describe their extensions.

As I have said before, language awareness develops early in life as adults comment to children about their movement. Language heard is soon language used, as children incorporate the words they hear for specific locomotor movements and extensions into their play conversation.

Suggested Activities—Body and Language Awareness Through Locomotor Movement

1. Suggest that the children spread out so that each child is standing on a carpet square or inside a hoop or on an X made on the floor with tape. *Note:* If you use a carpet square, be certain it does not slide easily, so that the children will not slip and fall. If you use a hoop, be certain it is large enough so children don't land on the rim. Say "Do this with me," and then begin jumping several times with two feet, landing each time on both feet. Encourage the children to join in. Stay on your carpet square or in your space as you do this. Then ask "Does anyone know what we call this movement? That's right, we're jumping. What is the body doing when we jump? Yes, we're using two feet to go up in the air and two feet when we come down." (*Note:* The label "jumping" is the *language awareness,* and the body landing on two feet is the *body awareness*). Encourage the children to try staying on their carpet squares as they jump. After a while say "Watch me and listen. Jump again, but this time say 'JUMP' each time your feet land." Then ask the children "When do I say 'JUMP'? That's right, Randy, when my feet come down. Can you all do that?"

2. Outside in the play yard, suggest that the children begin to gallop by saying "Can you follow me? We are galloping." Stop and ask "Can you gallop to the fence and back to me?" When you return ask "Who can gallop with the other foot as the leader? Look, Jane is galloping! Let's all try it. What do our feet do when we gallop? Yes, Zachary, they do run in a funny way. Where shall we gallop this time?"

3. Have the children stand apart in a large space. Ask "Can you balance on one foot as I'm doing? Can you balance on the other foot? Good! Watch me. Do it with me. Do you know what we're doing? We're hopping. Are we changing feet, or staying on the same foot?" (By answering your questions, the children begin to perceive that you are going up and down on the same foot, which is body awareness.) "Try hopping again. Can you hop two times? Three times? Four times? Who would like to show us a special way to hop?" The children's language awareness is stimulated by using and focusing on the word "hop" to describe the movement.

Developing Space and Time Awareness in Locomotor Movement

It's large-group time in the preschool. At small-group time the children were working with the concepts of short and long. Jenny, their teacher, now expands on these concepts by having the children walk with short and long steps. She says, "Who can walk with long steps? Who can walk with short steps? (The children spend some time walking in short and long steps.) "Jimmy and John, can you walk together with your long steps? Sally and Betsy, can you walk together with your short steps?"

It's large-group time and the children are working with the concepts of starting and stopping. Kathy, the teacher, says to them, "Listen to the music and plan a way to travel." (Different ways of moving are described by the children.) Then Kathy starts the music, and the children begin to move in the ways they have indicated. Kathy stops the music and says, "When you don't hear the music anymore, that is a signal to stop moving and make your body be very still. When the music starts again, choose another way to move. Now, what are you going to do when the music stops?"

Space awareness—understanding the "where" and the "how" of a movement—plays a most important part in executing locomotor movement because of the potential for bumping into people and objects when moving in general space. If there are a number of children moving at once, it is often a good idea for them to perform the four most basic movements—walking, running, jumping, and hopping—in personal space. However, opportunities to move in general space also are important and vital to developing freedom and ease of movement and the ability to control movement. Certain basic locomotor movements, such

as the gallop, slide, and skip, lend themselves only to moving in general space. Experience is the best teacher when it comes to children traveling comfortably and safely in general space and developing awareness of space.

One strategy to use with children who do not move well in general space is to have part of the group moving (stepping, hopping, running, jumping) in general space while another part performs the same movement (steps, hops, running steps, jumps) in personal space. Having everyone move in the same direction also promotes children's success when moving in general space.

Another useful strategy is to have half of the group of children on one side of the room and half on the other side, with the two groups facing each other. Then the children cross over to the opposite side of the room without touching anyone. Begin this game with walking, and then progress to other, more energetic locomotor movements, gradually increasing the speed with which the crossings are made.

Understanding where they are executing their locomotor movements in general space is part of children's space awareness. The major difference between a nonlocomotor and a locomotor "where" is this: "Where" in nonlocomotor movement describes the movement in relation to one's own body, whereas "where" in locomotor movement describes the movement in relation to an object, another person, or the space. "Where" in locomotor movement can be described by all of the same **spatial relationships** that we applied to nonlocomotor movement:

Children who have good space awareness can move fast in the large-group-time area.

in(side)/out(side)	**in front of/in back of**
around/through	**near/far**
between/alongside	**up/down**
over/under	**on/off**

Awareness of these spatial relationships allows young children to fine-tune descriptions of their locomotor movements: "I am skipping in front of Jack." "We're galloping around the field." "Let's try jumping over each red tile."

Locomotor movement **extensions**—which concern the "where" and "how" of locomotor movement—are similar to those for nonlocomotor movement:

direction	**level**
size	**pathway**
intensity (force)	**timing**

There are a variety of ways that these extension concepts apply to young children moving in locomotor ways.

Direction. The basic directions that young children's locomotor movement can take (often referred to as the *directionality* of movement) are these: **upward, downward, forward, backward, sideward, around,** and **circular.** If a movement involves using only one side of the body—for example, leading with one side while sliding—*laterality* as well as directionality is involved. Every movement a person performs has directionality that can be made conscious. Now let's consider each of the basic directions in relation to working with young children.

- **Movement can be forward or backward.** When young children travel through space, they generally walk, run, march, jog, tiptoe, gallop, or skip in this forward direction. Children also often like to experiment with traveling backward.

- **Movement can be sideward.** Traveling sideward is primarily done by sliding. However, children enjoy trying to perform the other locomotor movements in a sideward direction.

- **Movement can be around—in a circle.** Children can use any of the locomotor movements to travel around in a small circle in personal space or in a large circle in general space.

Level. As explained earlier in connection with nonlocomotor movement, the concept of level generally involves movement in three horizontal planes—*low, middle,* and *high.* For example, rolling and crawling are locomotor movements that are performed at a low level. Also, crouching the body toward the floor would permit the approximation of a low-level movement.

Though it is not possible to have the whole body at a middle level (defined as the level between knees and shoulders when standing upright), one can do locomotor movement and place the arms, head, or one leg at middle level.

(Generally, we don't use the more subtle middle level with preschoolers—just high and low, which are very pronounced movements and easy for young children to distinguish.)

Similarly, moving at a high level (defined as "shoulder height and above" when standing upright) is difficult for the whole body, but high-level movement can be approximated by jumping and drawing the knees up. Stretching and reaching both hands straight up is another way to bring parts of the body to a high level with movement. Walking on a balance beam is one way for a child to do this.

Size. While moving in locomotor ways, children can vary the size of their steps or jumps or hops, making them *large, medium,* or *small. Big* and *little,* or *long* and *short,* are other terms often used for these size extensions in locomotor movement.

Pathway. As with nonlocomotor movement, the pathway of a locomotor movement can be thought of as a *straight, curved,* or *zigzag* line that the body "draws" while moving.

Intensity. The intensity, or force, of locomotor movement depends on how much effort the movement takes, or the style with which it is performed.

Timing. Locomotor movement is affected by another extension—the **timing** of the movement. Timing—**time awareness**—is an essential part of locomotor movement. Therefore, it is not surprising that locomotor movement involves some of the same **timing concepts** that were discussed in connection with nonlocomotor movement:

starting/stopping   **fast/slow**

getting faster/getting slower   **even/uneven**

 ### Suggested Activities—Direction

1. Suggest that your preschoolers stand outside a large circle in the movement area and face the circle. "Let's try jumping into the circle and out of the circle. Can anyone show us another way to jump into the circle?" Next, demonstrate jumping in and out with your side to the circle, and ask the children "Can you do it this way? Can anyone show us another way to jump in and out?" (Children's space awareness is enhanced by experiencing moving in relation to a circular formation.)

2. Encourage the children to crawl around the room. Ask "Can you crawl backward? Can we find another way to crawl?" Try to have children explore crawling sideward or around in a circle. Ask "What parts of your body touch the floor when you crawl? Can you crawl with just your hands and feet touching the floor? What do you want to call our new way of crawling?"

3. Suggest that the children stand on one side of a large open area. Ask for four child volunteers who would like to plan a way to walk across the open space (for example, going forward, backward, sideward). Then encourage four more children to volunteer and suggest that those chil-

dren choose another way to walk across the space. Continue this activity until all the children have had the opportunity to walk across the space. Then say "Who would like to show us all another way we could walk across the space?" Continue encouraging children to explore until each child who wants a turn has a chance to be the leader and choose a way to walk across the space.

 ## Suggested Activities—Level

1. At outside time in the preschool, suggest that the children move about in specific locomotor movements and focus their attention on moving a part of the body at a certain level. For example, say "Try to put your nose up as high as you can while you walk around the play yard. What did you do with your head to put your nose up so high? Can you think of some other part of the body to put up high?" Then say "How can you move with your ear down low? What did you do with your body to put your ear so low to the ground? What else can we put down low?"

2. Have the children select two hand-held instruments they would like you to use as signals for high and low. For example, the children might decide that they want to move with their bodies crouched down (at a low level) when the drum plays, and with their bodies stretched as tall as possible (at a high level) when they hear the triangle. Play the instruments, and watch as the children move in the designated way. Children also can take turns signaling with the instruments. To extend this activity, ask the children to designate a different locomotor movement for the sound of each instrument, such as walking with the drum sound and skipping with the triangle. They might also choose a part of the body to hold at a given level as they walk or skip. This means the children must think of the locomotor movement and of keeping the special part of the body at a level, such as walking with the elbows low or skipping with the hands held high.

3. The following song can be used for a locomotor movement activity in the preschool. (The verse could also be recited as a poem, varying the voice level appropriately.)

Chant: 1, 2, 3, 4, 5, 6, 7, 8, STOP

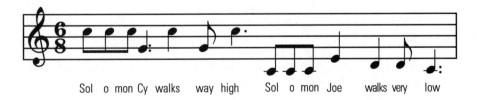

Sol o mon Cy walks way high   Sol o mon Joe walks very low

During the song, the children walk the way the song tells them to. Before the counting, they stop and each child decides which level (high or low)

was sung. Then on the counting, they begin to walk at that level until the leader says "stop." When they stop, ask the questions "How did you choose to move? Did you like walking like that?" The game can continue with the new locomotor movement chosen by the children. (Substitute the name of the new locomotor movement for "walks" in the song.)

 ## Suggested Activities—Size

1. Begin with verbal directions involving *size* and then show how they relate to *level*. Say "How small (little) can you make your steps when you walk? Can you now make the steps large (big)? What can you do with your body while you take big steps? That's hard to do, isn't it? What can our bodies do when we take little steps?"

2. Make a square space with four jump ropes of equal length. Then ask "How can we walk around this square? Jimmy is using big steps. Let's try that. Can you jump around the square using small jumps? Which was easier to do, the big steps or the small jumps?" The square may be made smaller with the use of only two jump ropes. Have the children explore movements of various sizes outside and inside the square. Large and small hula hoops can be substituted for the jump ropes to make circular shapes. Items can be stacked at different heights for the children to match with body height as they move about the area.

3. The children are exploring ways to move through spaces of various sizes by moving through narrow and wide doorways created with blocks or cones. Use this exploratory opportunity to ask the children to plan how they will move through the doorway or to recall how they went through the doorway. The children should be encouraged to use other concepts as well, such as direction and level.

 ## Suggested Activities—Pathways

1. A circle that is painted on the floor of the preschool classroom can provide a curved pathway for children to travel as they engage in locomotor movements. Challenge the children to move in various ways both inside and outside the circle. During outside time ask the children "Is there something out here that we could walk around? That's right, Michael, we can walk in a circle around the tree stump. How else can we move around the outside of the stump?" Encourage the children to use different locomotor movements and to add the concepts of direction, level, size, an so on.

2. Using large blocks, the children establish straight and zigzag pathways in the preschool. This is a good opportunity to ask "What is the difference between the two block roads? Yes, Abdul, one road is straight and one is crooked (or has a funny shape) It's a zigzag road." Encourage the children to walk on the pathways and to decide what kinds of steps they need to take to stay on each. Also encourage them to walk in different

ways alongside the pathways. Be sure to question the children about the ways in which they are walking on or near the pathways. Set up an obstacle course with straight, curved, and zigzag pathways. Other items in the classroom that could be used to construct pathways are carpet squares, the children themselves, rhythm sticks, paper plates, and chalk or tape markings on the floor.

3. Say to the children "Look around and see if you can find a straight stick in the room. Did you find something? Who would like to tell us what they found?" Children will volunteer. Then say "Plan a road to get to the straight stick and touch it. How are you going to move to your straight stick?" Each child can tell you how he or she is going to move and then can move to the object and back again. This activity can be repeated with other shapes, or colors, or letters.

 ## Suggested Activities—Intensity

1. With your support, preschool children can explore the meanings of words that denote a movement's intensity in this way: Ask "Did you ever carry something heavy? Enrico, what did you carry that was heavy? Can you show me how you moved with that heavy box? Let's all pretend we are carrying Enrico's heavy box. Has anyone else carried something heavy?" This activity can continue as long as the children are interested. Also, ask the children how they move while they carry something light. It would be useful to precede this activity with a discussion of what it is like to carry something heavy or light, with children actually trying to carry a light and then a heavy object.

2. Say to the children "Today all of you are very strong. Please show me how you can run across the play yard when you are feeling very strong." After they run, ask "What did you do in running to show you felt strong? How do you suppose you would run if you felt very weak? Let's try it. How did you move to feel weak?" Then ask the children to move in a strong way again until a prearranged signal and, at the signal, to freeze. Next ask them to move in a weak way until they hear a signal to freeze. Encourage the children to try variations in their movements. Let children take turns deciding how the other children should move and then giving the signal to freeze.

3. Suggest that the children explore the concepts of hard and soft by touching objects that are hard and soft. Then have them pretend they are one of the hard objects (like a block) jumping or a soft object (like a soft ball) hopping. After talking about the concepts some more and trying out different movements, have the children select two instruments, one as a signal for hard movements and one as a signal for soft movements. As each one is played, the children perform the appropriate type of movement. Whenever the playing stops, the children freeze and balance.

 ## Suggested Activities—Timing

1. Ask the children who are around you on the play yard to demonstrate moving fast and slow. Then suggest that the children copy you and tell you if you are moving fast or slow. (You are moving fast.) Encourage the children to try out fast and slow movements and then to describe their movements. Different children can be encouraged to volunteer to choose and lead fast and slow movements.

2. Ask "How many of you have ridden on a pony? Jermaine, can you show us what it looks like to ride on a pony? Let's all try that. If we are riding on a street and we come to a traffic light, and the light is red, what do we have to do? That's right, we must stop." Hold up two circles, one red and one green. Ask the children to pretend to ride their ponies when you hold up the green circle and to stop when you hold up the red circle. Invite the children to take turns being the leader and hold up the red and green circles.

3. The children in the preschool have made jello and know that it slowly thickens until it is solid. They also have seen what happens when they heat the jello and it turns into liquid. Ask the children to move about the room as if they were moving through a big bowl of just-made jello. Then say "The jello is beginning to get thicker. How are you going to move now? Oh, it's getting thicker and thicker!" The children's movements should be getting slower and slower. "The jello is *very* thick! Now it's so thick we are stuck! I'm going to heat the jello. It's slowly beginning to get more like water. Are you moving faster? Now it's back to the way it was when we first made it. What did we do when we pretended the jello was getting thicker? What did we do when we pretended it was getting more and more like water?"

Summary of Locomotor Movement

In locomotor movement the child transfers weight in personal or general space. Variations of these locomotor movements are virtually the same as the variations of nonlocomotor movement. When engaged in locomotor movement, the child is learning to use the body in many different ways: **body, language, space,** and **time** awareness.

Two important guidelines to keep in mine when helping young children develop comfort and awareness of locomotor movement:

*   During movement exploration, young children do not need to move with precise timing or to a common beat.

*   During movement exploration, young children do not need to be concerned about all starting at the same time or on the same foot.

The goals are to help children:

*   Develop an awareness of how the body moves about.

- Understand the language labels for locomotor movement.

- Develop improved balance, so starting and stopping can be achieved.

- Develop improved coordination and strength.

- Feel comfortable moving about.

Combining nonlocomotor or locomotor movement with objects, *moving with objects,* is the topic for the remainder of this chapter on **enabling the learner.**

During movement exploration children don't need to move with precise timing or to a common beat. They just need to have fun!

Key Experience: Moving With Objects

Objects can be combined with both nonlocomotor movement and locomotor movement. The key experience *moving with objects* is central to most sports and games. It includes all of the throwing, kicking, dribbling, catching, striking, hitting, and shooting that characterize these events. But *moving with objects* also includes movement with any hand-held object—not just those used in sports. These objects include paintbrushes, beanbags, scarves, bobbins, to name a few. If children have objects to use for movement activities, this provides opportunities for them to use motor coordination in new ways and to develop comfort with objects.

Children begin in infancy to move with objects. At first they grasp such things as rattles, shaking them without any particular purpose. Later on they focus on making an object do what they want—making a sound with it, or seeing and hearing it hit the floor as they drop it. A 1-year-old delights in pulling things out of drawers, banging on lids, and making stirring motions with wooden sticks in pots. By moving with objects in this way, infants are able to satisfy their curiosity. They often prompt adults to join them in games involving the objects.

As children enter preschool, they encounter other objects to be manipulated. They build with blocks, paint with brushes, dress dolls, play with sand and clay, push cars and trucks. Some movement with objects develops children's fine-motor control—sorting small objects, cutting with scissors, fastening with tape. In movement and music activities, children use scarves and paper plates and various rhythm instruments. Outdoors, they move on swings, tricycles, and scooters and climb through tires and over play structures. While children are moving with objects, adults are observing, supporting, encouraging, and guiding them rather than "teaching." We make comments and ask questions to stimulate children's **body, language, space,** and **time awareness** during these experiences. It is important that children, before entering kindergarten, have plenty of movement opportunities like those just described.

Young children's explorations with objects can provide time for you to observe and evaluate their various levels of motor development. For example, giving each preschooler in your setting a large soft ball and then watching what they do with the balls can be instructive. How do they try to toss and catch the balls? Do they try to walk over a ball, sit on it, balance it on their head, or put it on the floor and kick it? Your comments during these kinds of explorations can serve to highlight children's ideas and also give other children ideas to explore. Suggesting that a child try something another way, as long as the suggestion is not an intrusion, may expand his or her creativity: "Casey, you're balancing the soft ball on your head. Is there any other way you can balance the ball?" It is important to realize that the key experience *moving with objects* involves children's unique explorations with objects as well as opportunities for them to see object-use modeled by other children and adults.

When young children are given sufficient opportunities to use the body in nonlocomotor and locomotor ways, and when they are given sufficient opportunities to explore and manipulate objects, their ability to move successfully with objects will be greatly enhanced. They need lots of opportunities not just to manipulate objects on their own but also to find their own ways to manipulate them. For example, each child should have a ball or beanbag or a pair of rhythm sticks and be given opportunities for manipulating such items in an unpressured, nonjudgmental, and positive environment. If a child who is trying to learn to catch a ball is criticized or constantly corrected, the motivation to continue the trial-and-error practice may be greatly reduced.

The key experience moving with objects encourages children's unique explorations. These boys are having lots of fun exploring with pumpkin balls.

In this section we focus on the movement patterns involved in using a ball—tossing, bouncing, throwing, kicking, dribbling, hand-catching—as well as the movement patterns involved in using other objects such as rhythm sticks, bobbins, ribbons, scarves, paper plates, and beanbags.

The children and Phyllis, their teacher, are copying one another as they explore different ways of moving while holding large hoops.

First we will review some ideas for using small objects during large-group time or outside time and then present information and ideas about traditional throwing, kicking, striking, and catching skills—movement skills that are often thought of as physical education, sport, and game skills.

Scarves and Ribbons

Each child in the preschool has a scarf. Music is playing, and the children are standing in place, each using a scarf to "paint" a picture on a large imaginary canvas. Katie, the adult, says, "Try painting your picture with your other hand. Have you tried it with both hands holding the scarf?"

These preschoolers are involved in moving their arms in many nonlocomotor ways. The colorful scarves, which are 8 inches to 12 inches square, are enjoyable for children to use and can serve many purposes. For example, we can help children begin to develop their tossing and catching skills by suggesting that each child toss a scarf into the air and catch it as it floats down. (The children, of course, must have enough space in which to move freely.) Scarf activities can also help children identify colors.

Nonlocomotor movement variations (direction, size, level, intensity, pathway) can also be explored in scarf activities. Ribbons (about 3 feet long) can be used as an alternative to scarves. A child can hold the ribbon or scarf on one end and move it in space, or the ribbon or scarf can be attached to a short stick, such as a rhythm stick. Then the child may run with the ribbon streaming out behind (like running with a kite) or turn the ribbon back and forth, making pathways in the air.

Sam, the adult in the classroom, has the children exploring how they can move while holding their ribbon wands.

Suggested Activities—Scarves and Ribbons

1. Provide each child in the preschool with a scarf or a ribbon. The scarves should be of different colors. Give children time to explore with the scarves. Then you might ask "If you are holding a red scarf, what are you going to do with it?" When the children finish demonstrating their choices, ask "Who would like to show us how you moved with your scarf?" This requires children to recall their movements. Continue the activity by mentioning other colors until each child has had a chance to move. You can vary the activity by having the group that has just moved suggest a way the next group might move.

2. Each child should be standing in place, with a scarf or ribbon tied to each wrist. Provide time for them to explore the object. Suggest "Let's pretend we are painting a picture on a big piece of paper on the floor. Let's use both our arms and now let's make believe the paper is in the air in front of us. What else can we do with the scarves [ribbons] tied to our wrists?" Encourage different children to become the leader and suggest that everyone copy and talk about the movements chosen.

3. In the play yard, the children are in pairs, with each pair holding a large scarf between them. Encourage the children to explore different ways they can move together while continuing to hold the scarf between them. Then suggest that they talk about how they just moved. To foster other ideas, you might make suggestions like these: "Can you move with your bodies low?" "Can you move your scarf in big circles?" "Can some of you stand still and some of you move around?" "Who would like to show us another way to move?" "Who would like to tell us how they are moving?"

Rhythm Sticks or Bobbins

It is large-group time in the preschool. Each child is holding two rhythm sticks—one in each hand. They are marching around and making believe they are the conductors of the band they saw in a parade the previous day. They are doing this to "Soldier's Joy," from Rhythmically Moving 2, *which is playing on the CD player.*

By marching, the children are performing a locomotor movement, and by using their arms they are also performing nonlocomotor movement. The use of the object makes the nonlocomotor movement more complex because the children must make a spatial adjustment of the hands holding the sticks so that no contact with another person is made.

Short rhythm sticks are good objects for young and inexperienced children to use, because they are more manageable than a bat or racquet. You can have the children move holding one stick with both hands, holding a stick in one hand and then switching it to the other hand, or holding a stick in each hand.

The sticks should be light-weight and no longer than 18 inches. Sticks that are 10–12 inches long are even better for young children or the 18-inch sticks can be cut in half and the ends sanded. They should be .5–1 inch in diameter. The sticks can be painted various colors. For some activities, it is helpful to have each stick painted two colors, with half the length painted in one color and the other half, in a different color.

Paper towel tubes, rolled up and taped magazines, or similar tubes can be substituted for rhythm sticks. Try to find objects that are close to 1 inch in diameter. Another substitute for rhythm sticks is a pair of bobbins. Young children like to use these as drumsticks. (Chopsticks also are good for use as drumsticks and for making shapes.)

The children and their teacher, Ruth, each hold one chopstick with two hands and try different ways to move the sticks.

All of the variations described in the key experience *moving in nonlocomotor ways* can be explored by children holding rhythm sticks or bobbins. The sticks provide children with an opportunity to explore spatial relationships in a new way, since they are now moving an object in relation to the body rather than a part of the body in relation to another part of the body. The stick, or sticks, can be moved in front of or in back of the body, or placed next to the leg. The children can use the sticks to follow verbal directions or to imitate the teacher or another child in the same stages of aural, visual, and tactile/kinesthetic responding described in Chapter 2.

☀ Suggested Activities—Rhythm Sticks or Bobbins

1. At large-group time in the preschool, you and the children can play follow-the-leader with each person holding a rhythm stick in each hand. Touch the ends of the sticks to your shoulders and pause for the children to copy, then continue by touching the floor on either side of your body, then by touching your knees. Next, suggest that the children find a new place to touch with the sticks. Ask "What are you touching with the sticks?" When the children understand the game, you can encourage them to lead.

2. Each child holds one rhythm stick in both hands. First have the children explore what they can do, then have them try tossing the stick with both hands and catching it with both hands. Continue the activity by asking them to try to toss the stick with one hand and to catch it with both hands, or to toss with one hand and to catch with the same hand. They can be challenged even more if you ask them to toss the stick with one hand and to catch it with the other. You may need to advise the children to toss their sticks gently. This activity is most successful if children are seated. Have them say "catch" as they catch the stick. Saying "catch" focuses attention on the task at the moment the child needs to catch the stick.

3. Each child should have two rhythm sticks or two chopsticks, holding one in each hand. Oatmeal boxes can be used as drums. (Two paper plates turned upside down on the floor may be substituted.) Suggest that the children explore playing their drums. (Several children share and all copy.) Suggest that all the children try to hit their drums at the same time. Then ask them to beat on their drums first with one stick and then with the other. In each case, have the children try to establish a group beat. Once the group beat is established, you might begin a chant or song to the children's beat. The addition of the chant or song will reinforce the feel of beat. You might also try a sequence of movements. Say, for example, "Let's see if we can hit the drum two times with the sticks and then hit the floor two times." Once the children can complete such a sequence successfully, have them hit the drum one time and then the floor one time. Remember that young children will be most comfortable doing this sequence slowly. Other suggestions for sequenced movements can be obtained from the children. Also see "Moving in Sequences to a Common Beat," in Chapter 4 for more suggestions.

Paper Plates

Children in the preschool have decorated paper plates and now are participating in a group activity that Marge, the adult, has begun by asking "Can you balance the paper plate on your head? Can you walk around without the plate falling off? Where else can you balance the plate while walking around? I see people balancing the plate on their arms and on their faces. Sari has her plate on her shoe. Sari, would you like to be the leader? Let's all try Sari's way."

In this scenario, the children are using the plates for a balance activity. Other ways to use paper plates include the following:

- The children can hold one plate in two hands, one plate first in one hand and then the other hand, or one plate in each hand. They can be encouraged to follow your visual and verbal directions (see Chapter 2, pages 34–35).

- The children can use paper plates to further develop their awareness of nonlocomotor movement, such as described (see "Suggested Activities," below).

- Two plates can be used to define a child's personal space, in the same way that carpet squares are sometimes used. To do this, a child stands with each foot on a separate paper plate or with two feet on one plate.

- Two plates can be moved with the feet—plate dancing.

- The children can hit the plates together as if they were cymbals.

- The plates can be turned upside down on the floor and used as drums with the rhythm sticks or bobbins serving as drumsticks.

- Encourage children to suggest other ways to use the plates.

If the children are going to be moving the plates, it is easier for them to use 5-inch or 6-inch plates. If the plates are going to be used as targets or to define personal space, 8-inch or 9-inch plates are most appropriate.

 ## Suggested Activities—Paper Plates

1. Each child at small-group time holds a paper plate in each hand. Encourage the children to find ways to hit the plates together, to hit them on the table, and so on. Different children volunteer to be the leader for the group. Everyone copies the leader. You can suggest a word to match the steady beat of the plate movement, such as "TAP, TAP, TAP, TAP," and then suggest that you all try to keep the movement going and add the word.

2. If the preschool has a large area of smooth carpeting, or any other large smooth surface, you can show the children how, by putting a plate under one foot, they can use the plate as a scooter. First have children explore and share. Then ask "Where can we go with our paper plate scooters? Can we go in a straight path? Can we move around this circle on our scooters? Now we are moving on a curved path. Did you try to put the paper plate under the other foot? That's hard, isn't it? Do you suppose we can move around with a paper plate under each foot and do paper plate dancing?" For moving to music, you can provide instrumental music, such as "Sneaky Snake" from *Rhythmically Moving 4,* or any other music without words.

3. Encourage the children to perform free movements while holding one or two paper plates. A musical selection, such as "Southwind" from *Rhythmically Moving 1* or "Hole in the Wall" from *Rhythmically Moving 4,* can be used to encourage slow, flowing movements.

Beanbags

Each of the children on the playground has a beanbag. They are tossing and throwing the beanbags, and their teacher, Donna, decides this would be a good time to introduce some experiences centered around the concepts of up/down, high/low, and near/far. Donna gets the children started by saying "Watch me and copy what I do. Where did the beanbag go?" Donna tosses the beanbag up and lets it fall to the ground. Then she says, "Let's all try again." After the children have tried it several times, Donna continues the activity by asking "Can you make the beanbag land far away from you? Can you make it land near your feet? Where else can you make it land?" Children suggest in front of and in back of them.

The children are practicing tossing and throwing skills using beanbags instead of balls. The sizes of the beanbags may vary, but those 4 inches to 6 inches in diameter work quite well with young children. Each child in the group should have a beanbag, to avoid some children having to wait for a turn. Beanbags are versatile. They can be used for balance activities, for activities focusing on space awareness, for practice in catching, and as shakers to keep the beat in a singing game.

 Suggested Activities—Beanbags

1. Make sure each child has a beanbag. Place a basket (or box) in the middle of a circle in the classroom, and have the children toss the beanbag into the basket. Once the children are successful, you can encourage them to try to toss the beanbag in different ways, such as overhand or using the "other" hand, and from different body positions, such as with body low or while standing on one leg. You also can engage them in conversation about the ways they are tossing the beanbags and the positions they are using.

2. A variation on the singing game "Looby Lou" can be performed with beanbags. On the chorus, the children should walk around balancing their beanbags on a part of the body agreed upon in advance. They may be balancing them on their arms, singing "We are balancing beanbags (repeated three times) all on *Monday* morning." Substitute the appropriate day of the week for "Monday." The melody is "Looby Lou." The verse might be "We move the beanbag in. We move the beanbag out. We give the beanbag a great big shake and turn ourselves about!" Substitutions might be "We toss the beanbags in (children toss them to the center), we toss the beanbags out (children retrieve their beanbags and toss them out of the center)," or "We toss the beanbags up and let them fall to the ground, we pick the beanbags up again and turn ourselves around!"

3. You can give the children verbal directions, such as "Put your beanbag on your head, on one shoulder, on the other shoulder." Please see the "Stages of Aural, Visual, and Tactile/Kinesthetic Decoding" section on pages 43–45 for additional simple suggestions for verbal direction or visual demonstration.

Manipulative Skills With Balls: Throwing, Kicking, Striking, Catching, Dribbling

The children are playing with balls in the play yard. Some children are kicking the balls around the play yard and running after them. Some children are bouncing and catching the balls. Some children are trying to toss and catch the balls with others.

These children are engaged in a very natural manipulation of an object. The skills we most commonly think of as ball skills—throwing, kicking, striking, and catching—are ones that should be introduced informally during the preschool years. These skills require a child to tackle gross-motor movement while processing visual information. Thus they are engaging in a combination of visual processing and motor coordination activity. Infants begin to track objects visually and are fascinated by their movement. Infants soon learn that they can manipulate a hanging object by hitting it with a hand or with a foot. Later on, when very young children can move around more, they learn that

Phyllis, the adult, supports these children as they explore what they can do with the soft balls they are holding. They are placing the ball in various areas around the body, as well as using them to toss and catch.

they can throw objects, move objects around with their feet, and strike them with their hands. These throwing, kicking, and striking skills using stationary objects precede the more advanced catching skills.

Objects to use first for manipulative ball skills are scarves, balloons, or soft balls of 8 inches to 12 inches in diameter (these can be made from scraps of cloth and filled with polyester fiberfill). The commercial Nerf balls may also be used.

Although handling or manipulating a ball in some way is familiar to most everyone, comfort, coordination, and precise skill in ball handling do not come naturally to everyone. From the time that one first encounters a ball—perhaps as an infant or toddler—through school age and later, manipulative skills with balls are developing, being refined, and turning into mature movement patterns. A child gradually becomes able to use the hands and feet and then the whole body, as well as visual information, to successfully propel or stop a ball. Exploration is at the core of this refinement, and young children need lots of opportunities to become involved in activities using balls. Various terms are used to describe this *propelling* and *stopping*.

Amanda throws the ball at the basketball hoop as she has seen other children do, and she makes a basket!

Throwing. The easiest of the manipulative ball skills is throwing. The child holds the ball in one hand and propels it through space. The child can use an underhand, an overhand, or a sidearm motion. Most children pass through several developmental stages of throwing. When adults are not aware of these stages, they often have unreasonable expectations of what the young child should be able to do. They expect the child to throw like a big-league pitcher—bringing the ball back behind the head, turning the body, and stepping on the opposite foot. Instead, children need to explore in their own way.

Like other manipulative skills, throwing emerges from much imitation, trial, and error. Suggestions such as "Try to throw the ball farther" are useful. Later on, you might ask, "How can you throw the ball a different way?" Experimentation, exploration, and support are the keys to helping children develop comfortable and mature patterns of throwing.

Once a child throws comfortably, it is time to introduce suggestions about throwing for various distances, at a target, into a basket, over a net, underhand, or to a catcher. Introducing a different object for throwing, such as a Frisbee, poses a different set of challenges. Again, the child should have time for experimentation, observation, and imitation before trying to develop specific skills.

Noah's teacher gave him a sack stuffed with newspapers and suggested he find ways to move with it. Noah decided to play kickball with his friends as they moved across the playground. Tommy, on the other hand, in the photo directly above, has set up a pretend soccer field with his friends and is taking his turn kicking the "ball" into the goal.

Kicking. From a young age, children like to kick at objects that are in their path as they walk along. The first kicking skills to develop are those in which the child propels a stationary object through space with his or her foot. A child's first attempts at kicking a ball may seem more like a pushing motion, as the child stands still and tries to move the ball forward with the foot. Later on, the child will approach the ball and bend the knee more as the kicking motion becomes more advanced.

Because lower-body control lags behind upper-body control in children's motor development, kicking is more difficult for young children than throwing. At a certain point, however, it is natural for young children to begin to use their feet to move objects in their path. Their first kicking experience usually involves a stationary object. Before any kicking is taught, young children need many informal opportunities to kick a stationary ball with either foot. Gradually, as children use their feet to push rocks, sticks, tin cans, and other objects they may find laying on the ground, the pushing action becomes an action in which the knee bends. The traditional kicking motion emerges. After this informal kicking experience, more mature patterns develop. Children may take first a single step, and then several steps, as they approach an object with the intention of kicking it.

As with throwing activities, children need opportunities, apart from formal teaching situations, when they can practice kicking on their own. Compared to aimless kicking of a stationary object, kicking a ball at a stationary target, kicking a ball to a person who is moving, or kicking a moving ball are all much more difficult for young children, due to the visual tracking and processing of information that must occur for the child to be successful.

Striking. Striking, another form of the *moving with objects* key experience, is the third manipulative skill that can involve a stationary object. At first, the child can use a hand to strike a soft ball hanging from a string or rope, or to strike a ball placed on a tee. When a striking implement is introduced, it should be something like a paddle—an implement with a short handle and a large striking surface. This enables the child to realize success almost immediately. Long-handled bats, tennis rackets, and similar objects are difficult for young children to manipulate. With such implements, the long distance between the striking surface and the hand makes it difficult for the child to judge distance accurately.

The child's first striking movements are more of a chopping action than a twisting motion. Unfortunately, adults often try to place the child in a "batting position" before the child has had an opportunity to explore the nonlocomotor movements of rotating the body and swinging the arms horizontally.

When the child is ready to try to strike a moving target, it is best to begin with something light, such as a large soft ball, and to drop it rather than toss it to the child. A ball placed on a tee is stationary and more easily struck. When the child is ready to have the ball tossed, try to toss it accurately at the place where the child is swinging. When children toss to other children, they may not be able to throw with such accuracy, and this may lead to frustration.

Catching. Catching an object involves receiving it and bringing it under control. Catching is the most difficult of the early manipulative ball skills for two reasons: (1) the dimension of *visual tracking* is involved along with motor coordination and (2) children are often startled by objects coming toward them, which

results in them closing their eyes. Thus, young children should start off by catching scarves or soft balls, which have a slow rate of descent. Remember, if a child in your care has difficulty tossing an object, which would then create difficulty for the catching motion, you can simply drop the object in such a way that the child can catch it. Suggestions for introducing tossing and catching, in which the child is both the tosser and catcher, follow. Try them using a large soft ball, a large playground ball, or a beanbag.

- Toss from two hands and catch with two hands.

- Toss from one hand and catch with two hands. (Encourage the child to try tossing from the other hand also.)

Bouncing and catching can follow *tossing and catching*. When young children first attempt to bounce and catch a ball, most children will grab for it on each side as it comes up off the floor or ground. In the actual bounce and catch, however, the position of the hand must change. Bouncing occurs with the palm of the hand down, whereas catching occurs with the palm of the hand up. The child must wait until the ball comes above the hand and starts down before trying to catch it. This skill requires visual tracking that is new to the child. Occasionally, a child will be successful with this skill before being successful with tossing and catching, because in bouncing there is more time to prepare for the catching.

If the child you are working with is experiencing difficulty, try initially bouncing the ball for the child. The sequence for introducing bouncing and catching will be the same as that for introducing tossing and catching. Some children may toss the ball up in a way that makes catching it almost impossible. In that case, they may need to begin by just tossing the ball up with two hands and tracking it visually as it drops to the floor, saying a word such as "BOOM" or "BOUNCE" when it hits the floor. After doing this many times, they gradually develop some sense of how the ball descends and are then ready to try catching it with both hands as it drops. Eventually they can try tossing with one hand and then with the other hand, still catching with both hands. Later on, with a smaller ball, catching with one hand in a glove might be tried.

Saying "CATCH" when the ball reaches the hands may help the child to visually track the ball's progress and then recognize the moment when the ball needs to be caught. It is helpful to support children's early attempts by asking a few nonintrusive questions or making suggestions: "What will you try next time the ball is tossed?" "Does it help to say 'CATCH' when the ball comes to your hands?" Remember, though, that too-frequent corrections and directions from a teacher or parent, or coercion to practice catching, can be discouraging for children.

Dribbling. Dribbling involves striking an object repeatedly with the feet or hands. Children often perform primitive dribbling with their feet long before they can control the ball with their hands in a repeated fashion. We have all seen young children moving a stone along with their feet as they walk down the street. It would be more difficult for them to do this with a ball, because a ball tends to keep rolling away from them, whereas an object such as a stone can be better controlled. A soft ball of 8 inches to 12 inches in diameter is useful in a child's early attempts to dribble with the feet.

Preschoolers really enjoy moving with objects!

Dribbling with the hands involves pushing the ball downward, bringing the hand up still in contact with the ball, then pushing it again and again. The young child may have difficulty with dribbling, because it requires that he or she move with the ball in a coordinated motion. As the ball rises, the arm rises, and then the arm travels downward again as the ball travels downward. This arm action requires steady beat timing, which many young children do not possess. (This subject is discussed in Chapter 4 in the section describing the key experience *feeling and expressing steady beat*.) The sequence for introducing dribbling the ball with the hands is the same as that for introducing tossing and catching.

Summary of Moving With Objects

Preschoolers need lots of opportunities to move with objects. Practicing first by pretending to move with the object often helps the child. **No one ever fails when moving without an object.** Adults can strengthen a child's ability to move with objects by demonstrating without talking, by asking questions that make the child more aware of the movement, and by being supportive of the child's attempts rather than critical of the child's failures. Adults should avoid "teaching" the child, because the child often is not ready for that level of instruction. If children feel "put on the spot," they may give up without really trying.

The three **movement key experiences**—*moving in nonlocomotor ways, moving in locomotor ways,* and *moving with objects*— are designed to help children become comfortable with movement, understand how their bodies can move in personal space, how their bodies can move in general space, and how objects can be used in these nonlocomotor and locomotor movements. Young children need time to work on these movement basics. By the time a child enters kindergarten the basic abilities should be in place.

This chapter's discussion about **enabling the learner** has repeatedly mentioned the importance of children having opportunities to explore nonlocomotor and locomotor movement. In the next chapter these explorations continue as we look at **extending the learner** through the key experiences: *expressing creativity in movement, feeling and expressing steady beat,* and *moving in sequences to a common beat*.

Extending the Learner 4

Previous chapters have explained the five movement key experiences that fall within the **engaging the learner** and **enabling the learner** categories. This chapter focuses on the three movement key experiences in the **extending the learner** category, which will support children as they move ever closer to movement proficiency. These key experiences—*expressing creativity in movement, feeling and expressing steady beat,* and *moving in sequences to a common beat*—build on children's emerging physical abilities, body awareness, and knowledge of movement concepts. They also extend children's creative and rhythmic abilities, as is evidenced by the following observable results:

- Children who express creativity in movement are ones who implement their own movement ideas, make decisions about movement, and solve movement problems. They are comfortable with representation and creative expression. They understand how the body moves and how to vary movements, and they have the confidence to try something new.

- Children who feel and express steady beat are ones who have **basic timing** and can keep the underlying steady beat of a rhyme, song, or musical selection in both nonlocomotor and locomotor ways.

- Children who move in sequences to a common beat are ones who have **beat coordination** and can successfully sequence movements in steady beat, perform action songs and chants, and perform early childhood fitness routines.

Regardless of which form of movement children engage in, they will also use the three key experiences that involve ways to move: *moving in nonlocomotor ways, moving in locomotor ways,* and *moving with objects.* A fuller explanation of what these abilities mean will unfold as we discuss the three key experiences in depth, one at a time.

These boys are thoroughly enjoying feeling and expressing steady beat and moving in sequences to a common beat. They are also implementing their own creative movement ideas!

Key Experience:
Expressing Creativity in Movement

Promoting creativity in the child is intrinsic to the High/Scope *Education Through Movement* program. Adults using the program's **active learning approach, teaching model,** and **movement core,** as explained in Chapter 1, are the *facilitators* as children explore, plan, make choices, initiate ideas, lead other children, work cooperatively, and solve problems. Children's own creative ideas are valued and built upon in this process, thus enhancing their lifelong ability to make decisions, solve problems, and express themselves artistically.

Expressing creativity in movement is not a one-time experience. Creative movement cannot be "taught" at a specific time or place. Rather, it evolves over time when children are in the care of adults who consistently promote and support the kinds of activities described in the preceding paragraph. Emphasis on creativity in movement should not imply a lack of emphasis on mastering movement skills and techniques. There is room for both in a safe, interactive early learning environment.

The early years are the ideal time to establish what creativity means and how each child can be creative throughout life. Too often, creative movement is misunderstood and considered by older children and adults to be a threatening idea.

Hula hoops serve many purposes in creative movement experiences. These children are figuring out how their bodies can move while they remain inside their hoops.

Once children have developed comfort with and awareness of movement in personal and general space, once they have ownership of the concepts embodied in their movement and can extend those concepts, once they have the self-confidence and support to try something different, the road to creativity has been opened. Creative movement, then, is seen as something inviting and freeing; *it means taking something familiar and changing it in some way.*

We cannot expect children to suddenly, one day, *express creativity* if there has been no lead-up through many opportunities to express individual ideas and make choices. To promote the development of creativity in young children, adults need to be consistently open-minded and supportive of all attempts made by the youngsters. It is especially important to avoid judging a child's creative efforts or comparing one child's effort to another's. Such comments as "Isobel is being so creative!" or "I like the way Jackson is moving around the room" may cause other students to feel that their efforts are not creative enough or that the adult does not like what they are doing.

As mentioned in earlier chapters, when using the **separate** strategy of the **teaching model,** giving children verbal directions (rather than demonstrating or giving hands-on guidance) often leaves room for them to be creative. Without a preconceived idea of how a movement looks, each child can respond to verbal movement directions in his or her own way. Even when demonstrating a movement, however, you may wish to encourage some creativity with it. One way to do this is to preface your demonstration by saying "Here is one idea you might try before you think of other ideas."

Another way to get children started being creative is to say "If you find it difficult to think of an idea, look around and try another child's idea first." Creativity begins with imitation. First the child imitates what others are doing; then he or she thinks of a different way to perform the movement everyone is doing. Watching several children going down a slide on a playground, we often see this happen. At first each child copies the previous child; then someone thinks of a variation, a different way to go down the slide; then several children think of their own variations.

For some children, moving creatively comes naturally. When doing a movement that others are doing, they may suddenly think of one or more ways to change the movement. An adult might want to capitalize on such an occurrence with comments that extend the children's creative ideas or with comments that help the children share their ideas with others, who in turn might think of additional variations.

For some other children, however, creativity does not just happen. While we cannot *make* a child be creative, we can provide exploratory experiences and guidance that insures safety and builds comfort and self-assurance. We can help each child to understand that his or her movement ideas are valued. We can see that each child receives as broad a range of movement experiences as possible, including all extensions for each type of movement. If we provide children with opportunities to make choices and to share those choices, we establish early on that self-expression and creativity are a natural part of movement.

There are three basic categories of creative movement. We will discuss each of these categories and provide suggested activities for each.

It's outside time, and these children are happily exploring a maze they have created using cardboard boxes and existing structures. They're busy deciding how to move from one log to another and how to cross the makeshift walkway.

- **Representing.** The child moves "as if" or "like" he or she were an object, an animal, or a person that probably is not visible or present in the room or play yard at the time.

- **Problem solving.** The child is given some but not all of the "pieces" of the movement puzzle to solve. The child is provided the opportunity to explore.

- **Creativity with hand-held objects.** The child has an object to use for his or her creative efforts.

Representing

The preschool children have returned from a trip to the local apple orchard. Mei Lei, an adult in the classroom, has the children talk about (recall) the things they did at the orchard, such as picking up apples from the ground and picking them from the trees. Mei Lei says, "Let's pretend we are picking up the apples from the ground and putting them in our baskets. How do we put them in the basket? Who would like to show us how we

picked the apples from the trees? Haru, that looks just like what you did in the orchard. Did someone else pick apples in another way? Yes, Monetta, I remember that you climbed on a box to pick your apples."

In this scenario, the children are using creative representation to recall movement they used on their field trip to the apple orchard. When children use representation in this way, it is important to focus on experiences with which they are familiar, objects they know about, or animals or people they have seen, rather than focusing on an experience, a place, or an object that is unfamiliar to them—such as asking children in a preschool in Florida to pretend they are cross-country skiing. The movement of skiing in snow would most likely be unfamiliar to Florida youngsters, although there might be children in the center who once lived in a place where they could go cross-country skiing with their parents. One of these children could demonstrate the movement for the other children, and you could ask all the children to copy the child's movement, but they would not have the "feel" for the experience that the first child has. Water skiing might be a more familiar activity for the Florida youngsters to demonstrate.

This form of creative movement, which is a favorite of young children, involves reenacting familiar actions or happenings, or imitating the movements of various living things and creatures. Children might be asked, for example, to move *as if* they were catching soap bubbles, or to move *as if* they were flowers opening up, or to move *as if* they were cats sneaking through the woods. (Sometimes, without thinking, we ask children *to be* a tree or an animal or some such thing. Of course, this is an impossible task and should be avoided—we cannot *be* anything but ourselves!)

Especially for the young child, it is important that the event or thing or creature to be represented is derived from the child's concrete experience. If this is not possible, at least basing the representing on something read about or seen in a movie or on television is a good idea.

When children are engaged in *representing,* the adult's role is not only to support but also to extend the children's efforts by asking them questions that call attention to what their bodies are doing. Engaging children in this way, encouraging them to talk about their representations, helps to further develop their movement vocabulary and to make movement a conscious decision on their part.

Young children, in particular, enjoy dressing up as a form of *representing.* For example, Gayle, a young child, might choose to dress as a ballerina for Halloween and then decide to ask her teacher to play music so she can dance around. Because it is Gayle's idea to dress as a ballerina, the dancing may last a long time. If an adult had suggested that Gayle dress as a ballerina and dance, she probably wouldn't have been as interested or stayed with the activity for as long.

Remember, *the secret of engaging learners of any age in representing lies in choosing examples that they have some knowledge of and that are age-appropriate. If the children initiate ideas, so much the better!* If adults make suggestions, it's best to immediately begin to follow the children's lead once the movement begins.

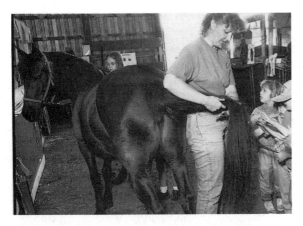

The day after an exciting trip to the county fair, the children proceeded to represent what they had learned from their experience. At large-group time they enjoyed moving like the horses, cows, sheep, goats, pigs, and chickens they had seen at the fair.

Jason has accompanied his older brothers to the local bowling alley and has watched them bowl. One day at work time, Jason decided to design and set up his own miniature bowling alley. He's intent on knocking down all of the "bowling pins" he has constructed!

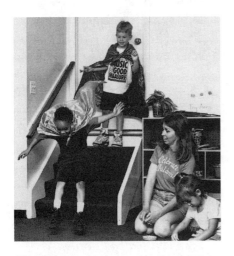

These boys are representing Superman, and they have donned capes and are trying to fly.

These girls are re-enacting scenes from a wedding they attended. The "bride," at right, and her "bridesmaid" are getting some hints from Julie, their teacher, on how to put on their pretend veils and then walk down the aisle.

After a trip to the local fire station, Dyani and Yuma are ready to put out fires! With support from their teacher, Kachina, they are preparing to use their "hoses" on their imaginary fire.

 ### Suggested Activities—Representing

1. The preschoolers have been to a parade and now are representing their experience by marching around the play yard. Jane, their teacher, says, "I found another way to march. Can you march the way I am marching? Who would like to show us another way to march? Lisa has an idea. Lisa, how do you want us to march? Let's all try Lisa's march."

2. A trip to the zoo can offer an excellent opportunity for children to recall the ways they saw various animals move and the sounds the animal made. Snapping photos of animals while at the zoo will help children recall their movements later. To start off this activity, encourage children to share their memories and then perhaps suggest forming an animal parade using the music "Peat Fire Flame" on the *Rhythmically Moving 2* recording.

3. The children have made popcorn and have watched the kernels explode. Ask "What happened to the kernels of corn in the beginning? What happened as they got hotter? Let's pretend we are the kernels of corn as we move to this music called 'Popcorn'" (from the *Rhythmically Moving 7* recording). Children will then represent the experience in their own way.

Problem Solving

The children are in the play yard. Some of the children are taking turns walking across a low balance beam. Jose, the adult, says to a child about to cross the beam, "Juan, can you walk across the beam with your body low?" Juan crouches down and walks across the beam. Other children want to try what Juan has done, so Jose waits for each of them to try the movement. He then says, "Can someone think of another way to move across the beam?" Carmen volunteers and walks across backward. Jose says to Carmen, "Can you tell the other children how you walked across the beam?" Carmen recalls her movement as she describes what she did. Jose then encourages the other children to try the backward movement.

As noted earlier, this category of creative movement consists of situations in which children are given some, but not all, of the "pieces" of the movement "puzzle" and are asked to solve the puzzle. A movement problem, or puzzle, can be made simpler or more complex merely by varying the number of missing pieces. This form of creativity is easy to ask of young children, if the "missing pieces" are kept to only one or two. The possible pieces to leave out are these:

- The *body part* to be moved

- The *type* of movement to do

- The *where* of the movement

- The *how* of the movement

- The *body position* for the movement (if applicable)

In the scenario about movement on the balance beam (above), Jose left out the *how* when he asked, "Can someone think of another way to walk across the beam?" The children knew the *body part* (the feet), the *type* of movement (walking), and the *where* (across the balance beam). Thus, Jose might have posed this problem to the children: "Use both arms in a slow bending and straightening movement." In this case, the *body part* (arms), the *type* of movement (bending and straightening), and the *how* of the movement (slow) are supplied. The children can decide *where* to do the movement. Jose could have asked the children *where* they chose to bend and straighten, and he could have made these additional comments:

- "How else might you bend and straighten your arms?"

- "What other body part could you bend and straighten?"

- "What other arm movement can we do slowly?"

- "What other position can we use as we bend and straighten?"

Problem solving is an effective way to help children develop their own creative movement ideas. It is one way to help children explore what they can do with each part of the body, with parts of the body in combination, or with the whole body, and how they can use the body in both personal space and general space.

Remember, in problem-solving activities, you do *not* continually provide specific directions such as this: "Swing your arms in front of you. Now swing them to the side. Now swing them down low." Instead, after offering an initial suggestion (for example, "Can you swing your arms in front of you?") encourage variations: "Now can you find a new place to

Evan solved the problem of how to walk across the hollow blocks that represent a balance beam. He decided to make two structures and then to put his feet on both to walk.

swing your arms? Are you swinging them fast or slow?" When children have not had much creative movement experience, providing the *how* or *where* of the problem to be solved may be very helpful as a starting point, as in the earlier example, rather than asking the children to supply these elements.

Here are some other problem-solving strategies adults can use to begin these kinds of activities:

- Ask if anyone would like to show what movement he or she is doing and then follow up by asking the other children to try the same movement.

- Demonstrate a movement yourself and have the children try it and describe it, before asking the children to suggest variations

There are many, many ways to encourage children's movement problem solving. The main objective is to have the children respond to open-ended questions rather than to specific directions.

 ### Suggested Activities—Problem Solving

1. It's large-group time in the preschool. Each child has brought a chair from the snack table to the area. The chairs are spread about randomly and each child hangs his or her symbol over the back of the chair. Encourage the children to move about the space, weaving in and out of the chairs, until they hear someone say "Stop sign!" When they hear those words, they freeze and listen for another suggestion for how to move back to their own chair and sit down. Gabe, an adult in the classroom, asks for a volunteer to suggest how all the children should move. Narmina, who volunteers, says, "Ready, go!" to begin and "Stop sign!" when the children are supposed to freeze. Gabe then encourages Narmina to give another suggestion for how children could move to return to their chairs. (Music may be added for this activity, perhaps "Bele Kawe" on the *Rhythmically Moving 3* recording.)

2. Preschoolers are about to move from the greeting area to their table for planning time. For this transition time, Dolores, one of the two adults in the room, suggests that each child move to the planning-time table by jumping with big jumps. Children are encouraged to share with the adults their plans for what pathway they will take, and then they travel to their planning table with big jumps. After all have arrived, the adults encourage the children at each table to briefly talk about what pathway each of them took.

3. At large-group time, play the musical selection "Southwind" from the *Rhythmically Moving 1* recording. Then suggest ways for the children to move to the music while they are seated. For example, ask "Can you move your arms slowly? Now move only one arm slowly. Can you move the other arm slowly?" Stop the music and start over so the children can explore other ways to move to the music while seated. Ask individual children for ideas on how everyone might move to the music. Keep

encouraging the children to make additional suggestions until everyone who wants to has participated. Each time there is a new leader, start the music again at the beginning of the selection.

Creativity With Hand-Held Objects

The children in the preschool have been given scarves. The musical selection playing on the tape player is "Gaelic Waltz" from the Rhythmically Moving 1 *recording. Rosie, the adult, suggests that the children listen to the music and then move their arms while holding the scarves with both hands.*

As in the example just presented, adding hand-held objects to movement is a strategy that enables children to move creatively. Often young children do not think that other children are watching their movements when they are holding an object, and thus they feel free to experiment. Objects can be used for either non-locomotor or locomotor movement.

A number of objects are suitable for creative movement. Colorful scarves, small paper plates, beanbags, and ribbons are but a few of the possible objects to use for encouraging *creativity with hand-held objects*. Using the instrumental selections on the *Rhythmically Moving* recordings, or other recordings, can provide many opportunities for creative movement with and without objects.

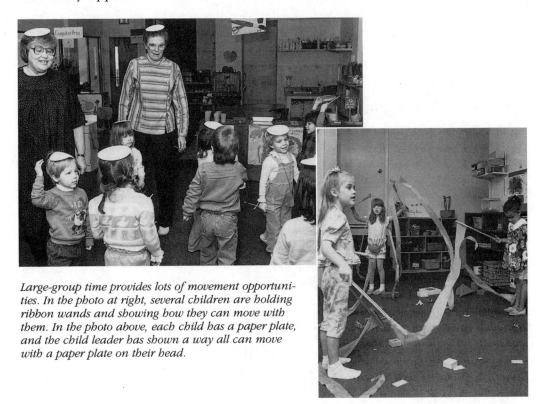

Large-group time provides lots of movement opportunities. In the photo at right, several children are holding ribbon wands and showing how they can move with them. In the photo above, each child has a paper plate, and the child leader has shown a way all can move with a paper plate on their head.

 ## Suggested Activities—Creativity With Hand-Held Objects

1. Give each child two short sticks (you could cut rhythm sticks in half and sand the end for this purpose). Encourage them to explore what they can do with their sticks. Chris, the adult, asks someone to share a way he or she moved with the sticks. All copy and then tell the leader about the way they moved. Encourage the children to continue sharing their ideas about moving in this way.

2. Each child is holding a soft pumpkin ball and is exploring ways to move the ball to different places while holding onto the ball. Chad exclaims, "Look, Suzanne, I am making my ball go up and down!" Suzanne encourages the other children to copy Chad. Another child says, "Mine is going in a circle." Suzanne tries to get the children to talk about what they have to do to make the ball go up and down or in a circle. Many other ideas are shared, copied, and talked about.

3. Children hold a beanbag in each hand and try to figure out how they can move with them. After providing a little time to explore, Michael, one of the adults, begins to put the beanbags on different body parts, pausing after each move (see "Stages of Responding" in Chapter 2). The children, seeing him do this, begin to copy. Soon Amanda says, "Watch me!" Amanda begins to lead as Michael has been leading. Pretty soon other children want a turn. Michael then begins to give verbal directions without demonstrating, and the children process and respond to his verbal directions. Lauren begins to do as Michael has done, giving verbal directions. The children are showing creativity by their choices for placement of the beanbags. This activity could be extended with action words, such as *shake* the beanbags in front of you, or *rub* the beanbags down your legs.

Summary of Expressing Creativity in Movement

Creativity with movement—the ability to take something familiar and change it in some way—is promoted, supported, and extended in young children when adults support their explorations, choices, initiation of ideas, leadership, cooperation, and problem solving. We have considered three forms that creative movement can take: *representing* (in which children represent, or reenact, movement of something or someone that they have seen or experienced), *problem solving* (in which children are given a movement "puzzle" with one or more of the pieces missing), and *creativity with hand-held objects* (in which children use objects for their creative movement ideas).

For any form of *expressing creativity in movement,* the essential ingredients for success are these:

*   Supportive adults who recognize children for their creative efforts

*   An absence of judgmental comments that can lead children to compare themselves with one another or to try to be "correct"

- Opportunity for children to begin creative efforts with imitation and to gradually branch out with original ideas

- Techniques and suggestions that are age-appropriate

The key experience *expressing creativity in movement* builds on each of the key experiences considered in earlier chapters. As the rest of this chapter will show, **extending the learner** also involves the remaining key experiences in movement—*feeling and expressing steady beat* and *moving in sequences to a common beat*.

Creativity in movement takes many forms, as exemplified in the actions of these children and adults!

Key Experience:
Feeling and Expressing Steady Beat

The movement key experience *feeling and expressing steady beat* is fundamental to both movement and music activities and is therefore also listed as one of the preschool music key experiences. Being able to *feel, express,* and then *keep* steady beat—the ability that we call *basic timing*—is one of the important prerequisites for early success in education. A child with basic timing is able to *independently identify* (feel) a steady beat; *express* the beat with both nonlocomotor and locomotor movement; and *keep* the beat throughout the rhyme, song, or musical selection. Basic timing is important because it affects, for example, motor skills, sport skills, musical performance, speech-flow, reading comprehension, and attention span. It is one of the most primitive and yet the most overlooked of foundational abilities.

What Is Steady Beat?

Steady beat is the consistent, repetitive pulse that lies within every rhyme, song, or musical selection. This pulse has even durations, occurs at equal intervals, and can be either fast or slow. In rhymes, songs, and musical selections, steady beat

It's large-group time, and this child is standing in the middle of the circle leading steady beat by patting his head. At left, Timothy suggests that everyone pat steady beat on their knees. He says delightedly, "Let's try it!"

is referred to as *microbeat* and *macrobeat,* which are terms used by Dr. Edwin Gordon (1984), a highly respected music learning theorist. To clarify these terms, let's consider two examples of steady beat—one involving a rhyme and one involving a song.

In the following well-known rhyme, certain syllables are underlined to indicate where one can feel a steady beat occurring:

<u>Hump</u>ty <u>Dump</u>ty <u>sat</u> on a <u>wall.</u>

<u>Hump</u>ty <u>Dump</u>ty <u>had</u> a great <u>fall.</u>

<u>All</u> the king's <u>horses</u> and <u>all</u> the king's <u>men</u>

<u>Could</u>n't put <u>Hump</u>ty to<u>geth</u>er a<u>gain.</u>

When students are learning to keep steady beat, they will often try stepping or walking to a steady beat such as the one shown by the underlining in the "Humpty Dumpty" rhyme. They take a step for each underlined syllable or word as the rhyme is recited. This steady beat is the **microbeat** of "Humpty Dumpty."

In any rhyme, song, or musical selection, there is another steady beat called the **macrobeat,** which organizes groups of 2 or 3 microbeats. It coincides with the first beat in each group of 2 or 3 microbeats. For example, in "Humpty Dumpty," this macrobeat organizes groups of 2 microbeats. To indicate where the macrobeat occurs, certain underlined syllables of "Humpty Dumpty" are now shown in boldface:

<u>Hump</u>ty <u>Dump</u>ty **<u>sat</u>** on a <u>wall.</u>

<u>Hump</u>ty <u>Dump</u>ty **<u>had</u>** a great <u>fall.</u>

<u>All</u> the king's <u>horses</u> and **<u>all</u>** the king's <u>men</u>

<u>Could</u>n't put <u>Hump</u>ty to**<u>geth</u>**er a<u>gain.</u>

Just as they are eventually able to feel the steady microbeat, children can also learn to feel the steady macrobeat of a rhyme, song, or musical selection. Chart 4.1 (for "Humpty Dumpty," see page 124) illustrates both concepts of steady beat—the macrobeat and the microbeat of rhymes, songs, and musical selections. The diagram is made up of units called *beat boxes,* with each beat-box representing a single microbeat. The beat-boxes with darker outlining and a musical accent (>) above them represent the macrobeat.

An example of a macrobeat that organizes groups of 3 microbeats can be found in the familiar song *America.* The beginning of *America* is shown here with the underlining showing syllables on the microbeat; the boldfacing indicates syllables on the macrobeat.

<u>My</u> <u>coun</u>-<u>try,</u> **<u>tis</u>** __ of <u>thee,</u>

<u>Sweet</u> <u>land</u> <u>of</u> **<u>li</u> -** ber-<u>ty,</u> . . .

For microbeat or macrobeat to be felt and expressed, movement such as rock-ing or patting the knees or stepping to the beat is the necessary ingredient.

What Is Rhythm?

The words and syllables of a rhyme and the note values in music create the **rhythm.** Rhythm is superimposed on the steady beat of the rhyme or song. As for the words of a rhyme or song, some are sung or chanted quickly, some slowly; one or more word syllables may occur within a macrobeat or microbeat. *This "surface action" of the notes and words within and among the beats is known as the* rhythm *of the rhyme or song.* A beat can be silent, such as the fourth microbeat of the first line in "**Peas** <u>Por</u>ridge **Hot** ___." Rhythm would be every syllable patted and no pat on the final

PAT PAT/PAT PAT

beat: "<u>Peas</u> <u>Por</u> <u>ridge</u> <u>Hot</u>."

Children's ability to feel steady beat makes synchronization possible—allowing children to say a rhyme, sing a song, or move to recorded music. The abstract concept of steady beat underlies any rhythm pattern. Successful beat-keeping includes independent ability to consistently feel, listen, aurally attend, and respond *in a continuous way* to steady beat. Therefore, rather than starting children moving to the *rhythms* of musical notes or words (see Chart 4.2 for a comparison of macrobeat, microbeat, and rhythm), we need to begin at the beginning—by providing all children with experiences in *feeling and expressing steady beat* so they can develop the *basic timing* skill needed to make rhythms precise.

Chart 4.1

Microbeats & Macrobeats of "Humpty Dumpty"

>		>	
Hump	Dump	**sat**	wall

>		>	
Hump	Dump	**had**	fall

>		>	
All	hor	**all**	men

>		>	
Could	Hump	**geth**	gain

The Development of Basic Timing—Steady Beat Independence

How can children today develop **basic timing,** which is the *inner anchor for personal organization and response?* To develop basic timing, children need the guidance of competent teachers and parents (or caregivers) who provide many varied experiences within a safe environment. We need to appreciate the value of children becoming secure and proficient in *feeling and expressing steady beat.*

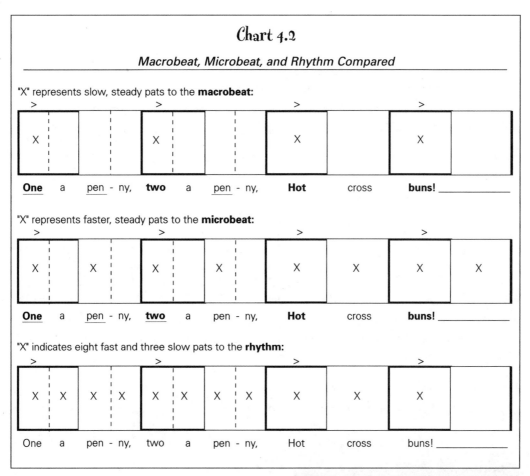

Chart 4.2

Macrobeat, Microbeat, and Rhythm Compared

"X" represents slow, steady pats to the **macrobeat:**

>				>				>		>	
X				X				X		X	

One   a   pen - ny,   **two**   a   pen - ny,   **Hot**   cross   **buns!** _____

"X" represents faster, steady pats to the **microbeat:**

>				>				>		>	
X	X			X	X			X	X	X	X

One   a   pen - ny,   **two**   a   pen - ny,   **Hot**   cross   **buns!** _____

"X" indicates eight fast and three slow pats to the **rhythm:**

>				>				>		>	
X	X	X	X	X	X	X	X	X	X	X	

One   a   pen - ny,   two   a   pen - ny,   Hot   cross   buns! _____

Unlike rhythm, which involves reading notes or words that one can follow, steady beat is abstract and requires keen listening and feeling to detect. Because keeping steady beat is one of the most fundamental abilities for learners of *any* age, it needs its own separate identity and task focus. *Moving to steady beat* should be the first thing that a child experiences, and *moving to rhythm* should follow only after basic timing is secure, (approximately by third grade). Beginning with movement response to rhythm before children can move to steady beat skews the focus (see Chart 4.3 for an illustration of this point).

Guidance leading to steady beat competence should begin very early indeed. When a pregnant mother sings or listens to music and moves to the beat,

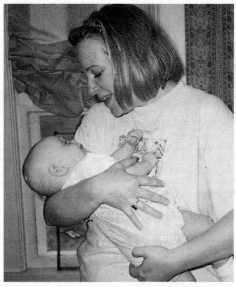

Christy is rocking her infant, Caitlin, to music played on the stereo. This movement helps Caitlin begin to develop the hearing-feeling connection.

Chart 4.3

Steady Beat Comes First—Joy to the World

It is an all too common sight to see a parent and young child listening to music, with the parent patting out the *rhythm* on the child's knee, hands, back. For example, we saw a mother, who herself had a good sense of steady beat, patting her baby to the *rhythm* of "Joy to the World." This means that she patted one long pat for "Joy," then two short, light pats for "to" and "the," and then a stronger pat for "world," and so on. The beat-box diagram for her patting would look like this (each "X" represents a pat):

Rhythm patting

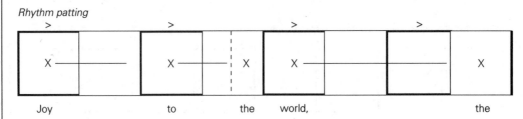

| | Joy | | to | the | world, | | | the |

If that same mother had instead patted or rocked the *steady beat* for the song, her stepping or rocking would look like this:

Microbeat stepping

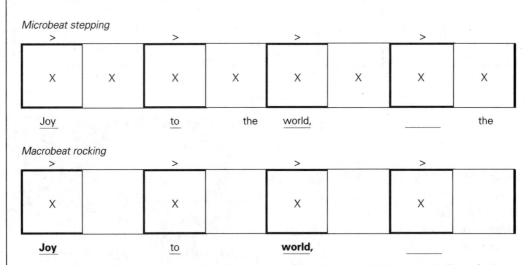

Macrobeat rocking

Precise rhythm patterns, far more complicated to perform than steady beat, are built on feel of steady beat—which is the first experience a child needs.

---

the infant in the uterus also is able to sense or feel the beat. Researchers tell us that the baby hears during the last trimester of pregnancy, so the hearing-feeling connection has already begun before birth.

During infancy, when the mother rocks, pats, and strokes her baby to a steady beat while saying a rhyme, singing a song, or listening to music, these nurturing actions continue to anchor this all-important concept—the feeling of a consistent steady beat linked to the rhythm of the speech. Throughout infancy and the toddler years, the child's growing strength allows him or her to engage in repetitive, steady-beat movements, such as shaking a rattle, patting the high-chair tray, or pounding with a toy. Adults can reinforce this timed movement by saying "PAT, PAT, PAT, PAT" or "BANG, BANG, BANG, BANG" to the steady beat of the child's movement. Bouncing the child on the knee while chanting a rhyme, dancing around the room to music on the stereo while holding the child, or continuing to rock the child while singing a lullaby all enable the parent or caregiver to reinforce the child's feeling for steady beat from birth to age 2.

Between ages 2 and 4, when children's speech is rapidly developing, consistent beat-keeping experiences are important for developing articulate speech flow. This is when the child needs to experience a great variety of steady beat movement responses linked to natural speech. This is the process whereby steady beat eventually becomes automatic. During the preschool years (and kindergarten as well), children need opportunities to experience a variety of repetitive single movements that lend themselves to beat-keeping: pounding, hammering, sawing, marching, jumping, swinging, rocking, tapping, and so on. We can reinforce any of these child-initiated steady-beat actions by saying "TAP, TAP, TAP, TAP" or "STEP, STEP, STEP, STEP" in time to the child's movement. The preschooler who has an abundance of experiences like those just described will be secure with steady beat before entering kindergarten. In fact, a child should demonstrate ability to independently feel and express steady beat by age 3.

These three children are able to walk together to the steady beat.

Each of us has a natural, internal steady beat. Most but not all of us can perform repeated, evenly timed, steady movement, such as patting our knees or stepping to our own steady beat. This internal beat may be slow or fast and may change from time to time.

Moving to our *own* steady beat is one thing; moving to an *external* steady beat—set for us by another person or by a musical recording—is another. If the external beat happens to correspond to our own internal beat, we will be successful naturally. Otherwise, as noted earlier, we may not be successful until we have developed **basic timing** (steady beat independence).

Children develop basic timing in two stages. **The first stage is beat awareness.** At this stage children develop these abilities:

- Move to their own internal steady beat.

- Match a steady beat that is spoken verbally (MARCH, MARCH, MARCH, MARCH) or modeled visually by others (using the **separate** strategy of the **teaching model** described in Chapter 1).

- Perform nonlocomotor and locomotor movements to the steady beat.

- Copy a leader's locomotor movement to the microbeat or nonlocomotor movement to the macrobeat of a rhyme or musical selection.

The second stage in developing basic timing (steady beat independence) is beat competence. At this stage children develop these abilities:

- *Independently* identify (feel), express, and keep the macrobeat in upper-body movements or step the microbeat in place.

- *Independently* keep steady beat in nonlocomotor (patting or rocking) and in locomotor ways (stepping, marching).

At this stage, a child with beat competence could listen to a march, independently feel the microbeat *and* macrobeat, and then independently keep the beat either marching to the microbeat or patting the chest to the macrobeat.

Children who have achieved beat awareness and then moved on to achieve beat competence have developed basic timing (see Chart 4.4). They have developed the hearing-feeling connection. We often refer to such children as "timed."

Robert, the leader of this movement activity, is keeping the steady beat by patting his shoulders, and the other children and their teacher, Michelle, are following Robert's example.

Unfortunately, this all-important ability to independently feel, express, and keep steady beat does not necessarily come with maturation, as Greg's experience points out (see sidebar, at bottom right).

To develop this ability in preschool—if as infants and toddlers they have not been rocked to rhymes, songs, and musical selections— young children need many varied experiences to become secure and proficient in *feeling and expressing steady beat*.

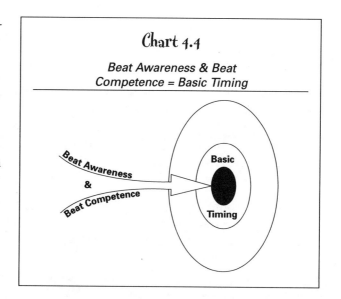

Building the Steady Beat Foundation— From Visual, Auditory, and Tactile Cues

There are specific ways to help children learn to follow a leader's beat. Be sure to employ the **separate** strategy of the **teaching model** (see Chapter 1). One way is to work with children's response to visual cues. The other way is to work with their response to auditory cues. At this point, the concern is not with being able to recite or sing—it is only with being able to watch and respond to or listen and respond to a steady beat

Responding to visual cues

Here are some strategies to use to evaluate and strengthen children's ability to follow visual cues for steady beat:

1. Either you or a child leads in patting with both hands or rocking a fairly slow steady beat (an approximate macrobeat tempo). Encourage the children to watch this visual cue and then join in by moving to the beat. When all are copying, the leader adds "PAT, PAT, PAT, PAT" or "ROCK, ROCK, ROCK, ROCK" to the action. Children join in with the word, if they can.

2. Either you or a child leads in a marching beat; after the children process this visual cue and join in, the leader says the words "MARCH, MARCH, MARCH, MARCH" simultaneously with the stepping action. Children join in saying the words, if they can.

Greg— A Preschooler Without Steady Beat

An adult riding in a preschool car-pool would often begin rhymes or songs the children had been exposed to in preschool. While doing so, she noticed that 4-year-old Greg seemed to have no sense of steady beat. The adult began using a hands-on guidance method of stimulating Greg in beat. While riding together, they would join little fingers and move their arms back and forth while singing simple songs like "Row, Row, Row Your Boat." Now, after 6 months of daily beat-keeping, Greg is just beginning to initiate his own steady beat to which the adult can respond.

Responding to auditory cues

Following are some strategies to use to evaluate and strengthen children's ability to follow auditory cues:

1. Either you or a child repeats a descriptive movement word in steady beat *without doing the movement*. For example, the leader might say "KNEES, KNEES, KNEES, KNEES" in a macrobeat tempo. The children listen to the auditory cue and join in with the movement of patting the knees, matching their patting to the timing of the words. As with the visual cues, some children may join in with the words matching the action.

2. Either you or a child begins speaking "MARCH, MARCH, MARCH, MARCH" in an approximate microbeat tempo. The children join in with the action, adding the spoken word if possible.

Responding to tactile cues

For some children, expressing steady beat is not easy. For them, tactile experience (hands-on guidance) may lead to success. The following are two successful strategies to use in supporting this experience:

Responding to visual, auditory, and tactile cues, the children at the top left are patting their heads to a visual cue; the two girls above are responding to an auditory cue as they pat their ears; and Ivan and Christie at the left are receiving hands-on guidance as Phyllis and Ruth, the adults, hold their hands and pat the beat with them.

1. Stand behind the child who needs assistance and pat him or her on the top of the shoulders. Encourage the child to try to match the "feel" by patting on the knees. This strategy works well if parents or other adults are present and can work one-on-one with the children.

2. When seated, try rocking to the steady beat with your arms around the children on each side of you, or patting on their backs.

Types of Movement Used for Feeling and Expressing Steady Beat

While children are learning to feel and express steady beat, use single movements. A single movement (such as "ROCK, ROCK, ROCK, ROCK") takes one beat to complete before it is repeated; one movement coincides with one beat. If a patting movement is used, remember the details of the **movement core** (see Chapter 1) and use two sides of the body (both hands patting knees). If a stepping movement is used, remember to alternate the feet in personal space. These types of movements are the easiest for young children to do. Rocking is an alternating movement and is an appropriate upper body movement for children who are learning to use steady beat while seated. The movement expressing steady beat should be made as silently as possible, to avoid giving auditory cues and to avoid having a child pull other children off the beat.

The beat awareness stage of developing basic timing (steady beat independence)

As noted earlier, the beat awareness stage is the first stage of basic timing (steady beat independence). At this stage, the child can keep *his or her own* beat, *match others,* and *listen* to rhymes, songs, and musical selections while *copying* the adult who is keeping steady beat. The child also can keep a steady beat while speaking a single word over and over or speaking a two-word combination, such

With Phyllis, their leader, these children are enjoying keeping steady beat on their teddy bears as they chant "Teddy bear" several times.

as "**ted**dy bear," giving one pat with the bold syllable. The child is not yet independently **keeping** steady beat. The stepping beat is closer to the child's natural tempo and therefore is the more natural beat for beginning beat-keepers, but the patting/rocking beat is most important and should not be ignored. Some children seem to have more success with this nonlocomotor beat because they are able to focus better when seated and when the beat is slower.

The beat competence stage of developing basic timing (steady beat independence)

Students need a variety of experiences using nonlocomotor movement with macrobeat to feel the organization of rhymes, songs, and musical selections, as well as experiences using locomotor movement with microbeat. For developing beat competence, some effective support strategies for the adult to use are these:

These children and their teachers are keeping steady beat as they tiptoe in place at large-group time.

- Suggest that children keep their movements silent (encourage them to use "spider" pats).

- Encourage children to choose their own way to rock or pat steady beat.

- Avoid always modeling the beat for children to copy.

- Use the steps for responding to visual/auditory cues on page 129.

The process for introducing steady beat using rhymes, songs, and musical selections

As children listen to more and more rhymes and songs, they begin to say aloud some of the words or to chime in with the pitches and words. The progression is as follows:

1. After children visually copy the steady beat that is modeled, or after they process and respond to the single word spoken with repetition (movement comes first), add an anchor word (a word used to help all children match the beat, such as "PAT" or "ROCK") repeated either four or eight times, and then add the rhyme. After a rhyme has been spoken a number of times, encourage the children to join in reciting the rhyme. It is important that you speak slowly enough for children to be successful, but at the same time maintain the *natural speech flow*.

2. If you wish to add a song instead of a rhyme, use an anchor pitch (the first note of the song) to give the starting pitch as well as the steady beat after the children are moving to the beat and before starting the song. The adult might sing "One, two, ready, sing" before beginning the song.

3. If you are using a recorded musical selection, softly say an anchor word to the underlying steady beat of the music during the introduction of the selection. Then drop this word once the introduction is over and children have begun moving to the beat. Again, remember that personal space is easier for young children to use than general space. Sometimes it is necessary to bring the anchor word in again if the children's attention slips or if they lose the beat for some other reason. Also, you may have to stop the recording. *A note about recordings:* Children will be more successful if the recording is instrumental (without words). Otherwise children may listen to the words instead of focusing on steady beat.

Remember, the progression for keeping steady beat is as follows:

- Doing the movement first

- Providing an anchor word or anchor pitch

- Listening to the rhyme, song, or recording while keeping steady beat, or "chiming in" with words or pitches of the rhyme or song, or speaking the rhyme or singing the song

Suggested Activities—Feeling and Expressing Steady Beat

1. Ask for a child volunteer to be the leader and to begin a simple patting movement for the other children to copy, such as patting the knees with both hands. Once the children are copying, begin to say "KNEES, KNEES, KNEES, KNEES." The children may speak with you. If most of the children are copying successfully, you then can add a rhyme or song that you keep to the underlying steady beat already established. The children stop saying "KNEES" and start to listen, "chime in," or speak. (If singing a song, sing "KNEES" using the anchor pitch.) Then encourage another child to set the steady beat by patting a different place on the body and then you can begin to SAY & DO (as explained in Chapter 2).

2. While seated on the floor, the preschool children can explore rocking motions—forward, backward, side to side. Talk with the children about rowing a boat, show them the rowing movement people use, and show them a picture of people in a boat. Then help the children arrange themselves in an imaginary long boat, with each child's legs alongside the child in front so the children are close together. They can begin to make a back-and-forth, steady-beat, rocking motion. After the beat is established, you add the anchor pitch with "One, two, ready, sing" or "One, two, ready, listen" and then begin to sing "Row, Row, Row Your Boat." Fit the *beat* of the song to the rocking motion established by the group. If the children have difficulty with the beat and motion, two adults could sit on opposite ends of the boat. This puts the children between the adults who can then guide the motion and steady beat.

3. Have the children sit in a circle. Begin singing the song "Paw Paw Patch," substituting the following words as the children pat steady beat:

   Jenny **mouse, walk** around the **cir**cle,
   Jenny **mouse, walk** around the **cir**cle,
   Jenny **mouse, walk** around the **cir**cle,
   and go **back** to **your place.**

   Then ask "Who would like to go around the circle and come back to their place?" Jenny volunteers. Ask Jenny how she would like to go around the circle. Jenny might reply that she wants to walk around the circle. Jenny can walk around the circle while the children sing the song. While singing, they should pat the macrobeat on a part of the body that has been selected by the group. (The beat is identified by singing the word that identifies the body part being patted before beginning the song.) The game is repeated with another child volunteering and choosing the type of movement. The child's name and chosen movement should be substituted in the song, for example, "**Cathy mouse, skip** around the **cir**cle." Be prepared to let every child who wants to volunteer have a turn.

Note: Good times for children to practice feeling the beat are while songs are sung, while rhymes are chanted, and while singing games are played—especially if there are times when some children are not active in the game, such as in the "Jenny Mouse" game.

Summary of Feeling and Expressing Steady Beat

Basic timing (steady beat independence) is the result of the key experience *feeling and expressing steady beat*. A child with basic timing ability can independently *feel* the underlying steady beat, *express* it with nonlocomotor and locomotor movement, and *keep* it throughout a rhyme, song, or musical selection. Basic timing underlies success with many tasks across curricular areas and throughout life.

In developing basic timing, a child uses his or her internal steady beat—which is usually **microbeat**—the natural walking beat. This is the first beat to use for marching or stepping. Young children also need to experience rocking, patting, and performing other single nonlocomotor movements to the **macrobeat**—the beat that organizes groups of 2 or 3 microbeats.

At first children keep steady beat by following visual and verbal cues provided by the adult or another child. Then they graduate to keeping steady beat while *listening* to single words and word combinations and matching single movements to the beat created. Then they move to the steady beat that is created as they chant words, recite rhymes, and sing songs. Instrumental music also provides steady beat for their marching, rocking, and patting movements.

As children have a variety of experiences that allow them to move from the first stage—**beat awareness**—to the second stage—**beat competence**—of **basic timing** (steady beat independence), they gradually develop ownership of steady beat. The ability to feel and express steady beat is essential to the final key experience under the **extending the learner** category: *moving in sequences to a common beat.*

These children, with their teacher, Michelle, are performing the easiest coordination movement as they pat their knees with two hands to the steady beat!

Key Experience: Moving in Sequences to a Common Beat

Mastery of steady beat—being able to independently feel, express, and keep macrobeat and microbeat—is most useful to learners of any age if they can extend that mastery from single movements to more and more complex movements that require greater body coordination. The mastery is even more useful, and enjoyable, if children can also extend it to performing various kinds of coordination-based movements not only alone but also in synchronization with others. Therefore, this chapter on **extending the learner** concludes with a discussion of the key experience *moving in sequences to a common beat.*

The result of this last key experience is **beat coordination,** which enables the child to sequence movements performed in steady beat, and to do so not only while alone but also with other children. Obviously, beat coordination is built upon and includes the general movement ability of **coordination** (of non-locomotor and locomotor movement) as well as the specific movement ability of **basic timing** (steady beat independence), discussed with the previous key experience. It is also fundamental to many important large- and small-muscle activities that a person encounters throughout life. Young children use beat coordination when they partici-

Children at large-group time are showing the "pizza" as they begin to sing the "Pizza Hut" action song. Another group also is showing actions with both hands as they sing.

pate alone or together in action songs and in singing games. Beat coordination impacts on basic sports abilities as well as on early childhood fitness routines, hand-jives, and dancing.

Changes in our daily lives—more sedentary occupations and recreation, less group and social interaction—may have cut down on occasions when beat coordination is developed or used. For many children, the inability to perform sequenced movements to steady beat precludes their participation in a number of daily activities that could enrich their lives.

In this section the focus is on helping young children develop the ability to sequence movement with others to a common beat. At first we will use nonlocomotor movements for this key experience because they are the simplest. (Please refer to the "Enabling the Learner" section in Chapter 3, for more information on nonlocomotor movements.) We will focus here on the nonlocomotor movements that involve choosing body parts or moving arms or legs (while seated) away from the body and that rely on one area of the body at a time, for example, arms (including hands), shoulders, trunk, legs (including feet). (When children use their legs they will not be standing, thus they will be engaging in nonlocomotor movements instead of weight-bearing locomotor movements.) You will find it useful to provide opportunities for this key experience during large-group time or as a transition activity to planning time or recall time.

What Are "Sequences?"

Since this last key experience has to do with "moving in sequences," we first need to explain what we mean when we use the word "sequences." Recall that in Chapter 1, in the explanation of the **movement core,** "sequences" refers to two or more purposeful movements joined together. So a sequence combines two or more purposeful movements; once these are completed, the sequence is repeated. These movements generally are timed, so steady beat comes into play. One example of a sequence is touching knees (the first movement), and then touching shoulders (the second movement).

Keep in mind, however, that sequences can be longer than two movements. Consider, for example, the sequences involved in the action songs, "Hokey Pokey" and "Eensy Weensy Spider." Both of these songs have movement followed by another movement, but the movements do not repeat in the same order. Another example, "Little Green Frog," has a 2-beat sequence that is repeated eight times—hands touch the floor and then lift up off the floor (for JUMP, UP). All of these songs, and more, are presented in *Movement Plus Rhymes, Songs, & Singing Games* (Weikart, 1997)

When working on beat coordination, it is important to be aware of the ease or difficulty with which students can perform various kinds of sequenced movements. For example, the easiest sequences are those that involve the arms in nonlocomotor movement (bending and then straightening the arms, or patting the head with both hands and then patting the shoulders). If a hand-held object is added to an arm sequence, it makes the sequence a little more difficult. The sidebar, on page 138, describes how one adult noticed a preschooler's attempts to sequence movement and then reinforced these attempts in a nonobtrusive manner.

A sequence has been started with children holding their arms straight; then the children will bend their arms.

Clearly, as children work toward beat coordination, the learner SAY & DO process can be used to help them learn to sequence movements. This process is reflected in the example of children touching knees and then shoulders—the children say "KNEES, SHOULDERS, KNEES, SHOULDERS" while they are doing the movement. This SAY & DO process gives children a way to combine visual or auditory information with cognitive processing in order to respond quickly and accurately. It enables them to think about what they are doing as well as to relate to movements someone else is demonstrating.

Using the SAY & DO process has been the route to success for children who lack beat coordination, just as it can be for children as they progress through the **levels of beat coordination** presented here. It is advisable to have children watch the movement demonstrated before trying to join in the movement itself. Having this "processing time" before starting the movement leads to positive results.

The **levels of beat coordination** for preschoolers are Levels I through IV. An additional two levels, V and VI, are not discussed here but are appropriate for children who are in second grade and above.[1]

Timmy Uses Sequenced Movements

One spring day, during outside time in a preschool, Jessie, an adult, was pushing 4-year-old Timmy on the swing. She noticed that his legs were beginning to perform the bending and straightening motion used in pumping. She began to reinforce Timmy's natural movement with language, saying "BACK" as his legs went back and "OUT" as his legs went out. As Timmy felt the timing of the words, his movements became larger and more pronounced, and he moved to the steady beat. From that day on, Timmy was able to pump himself on the swing.

---

[1]To find out about these two levels, see either, *Foundations in Elementary Education: Movement* (Weikart & Carlton, 1995) or *Teaching Movement & Dance* (Weikart 1998).

Because one can be a beginner in movement at any age, the information we present here about the four **levels of beat coordination** for young children can be used with older learners as well. That is, the first four levels are for preschool children or "beginning" learners of any age. Of course, movement examples should always be age-appropriate.

As we explain Levels I–IV of the **levels of beat coordination,** you may want to occasionally refer to Chart 4.5 to see the overall picture of combining the SAY & DO process with movement to achieve beat coordination.

Chart 4.5

Combining the SAY & DO Process With Movement to Achieve Beat Coordination at Levels I—IV

	Level I: Single Movement	Level II: Single Alternating Movements	Level III: Sequenced Movements	Level IV: Sequenced Movements Combined
SAY & DO	Unite language and movement. Both hands *or* both feet used simultaneously. "KNEES, KNEES, KNEES, KNEES" or "BOUNCE, BOUNCE, BOUNCE, BOUNCE"	Unite language and movement. Alternate hands *or* feet. "KNEE, KNEE, KNEE, KNEE" or "WALK, WALK, WALK, WALK"	Unite language and movement. Both hands *or* both feet used simultaneously. "HEAD, SHOULDERS, HEAD, SHOULDERS" or "WAIST, KNEES, WAIST, KNEES"	Unite language and two Level III movements. Both hands *or* both feet used simultaneously. "HEAD, SHOULDERS, WAIST, KNEES

Guidelines for Initiating the Levels of Beat Coordination

The guidelines for presenting the **levels of beat coordination** are as follows:

1. Have the children try out a movement by themselves with SAY & DO before having them do the movement with others. They are "trying it on for size."

2. Keep the time children are individually trying out the movement very short, so the children do not lose interest.

3. Be certain to include the children's suggestions of what body part to pat or what action word to use. The child who makes the suggestion will be the leader and will provide the SAY & DO.

4. Begin with movements in which children use two hands to touch the body or the floor, so that there is an endpoint to correspond with each word or beat, before using such movements as bending and straightening. In the latter movements there is no tactile endpoint to correspond with the beat.

5. Use only one area of the body at a time such as the arms alone or the legs alone in nonweightbearing positions. It is very difficult for young children, or beginners of any age, to move more than one part of the body at a time.

6. The block of time used when the children do movement together should be short; 1–3 minutes is generally recommended. If the children seem disinterested, stop the activity and go on to something else; then return to the activity later on. If the children are having fun, continue the activity for as long as desired.

7. Try to incorporate music as often as possible with the activity. The instrumental music selections on the *Rhythmically Moving* recordings provide a well-defined beat. Again, do not spend too much time on this activity, so the children don't lose their concentration. Suggestions for specific coordination activities are presented in *Movement Plus Music: Activities for Children Ages 3 to 7* (Weikart, 1989).

8. Remember to *demonstrate* without *describing* the movement you want the children to do, or *describe* without *demonstrating* what you want them to do. (Refer to the **teaching model** discussion in Chapter 1 and the key experience *acting upon movement directions* section in Chapter 2 for details on how to do this.) Note that the SAY & DO method (*one word spoken simultaneously with the movement*) *does not imply describing with phrases and sentences while doing*. Add the SAY & DO after the children have practiced the movement.

As noted earlier, the **levels of beat coordination** are presented in order, ranging from the simplest single steady beat movements to sequenced movements that are more difficult to coordinate. The sidebar on the facing page offers an example of how to present a Level III activity using the **levels of beat coordination.** Next we will examine each of the levels in turn.

Levels of Beat Coordination

Level I: Single movement

Children use the same single movement in repetition, using both sides of the body simultaneously. Example: Touching the knees repeatedly, saying "KNEES, KNEES, KNEES, KNEES" as they do so. A variation would be to use one side of the body in repetition.

This is the easiest of the levels because it uses one movement repeatedly. This single movement is the same level of movement used for developing basic timing (steady beat independence), in connection with the previous key experience. In the **movement core** it is the nonlocomotor movement, two sides, single. The tempo of the movement approximates the macrobeat.

Using learner SAY & DO is critical for success. Even when children are not yet able to feel, express, and keep the beat of a rhyme, song, or musical selection, they are able to do Level I movement repeatedly when learner SAY & DO is used. The movement eventually is performed simultaneously with the spoken word, thus creating the cognitive-motor link.

When working at this level with young children, it is better to use a single movement that has some tactile endpoint (the knees can be the tactile endpoint for patting, for example), rather than a single movement "in the air," such as "SHAKE." Younger children usually find it easy to use the name of a body part as the word they match with movement. One child can be leader, setting the beat by patting his or her head. The other children join in with the visual model, and then the leader adds the label "HEAD, HEAD, HEAD, HEAD," creating learner SAY & DO.

Another child may suggest a new movement, patting the ears. The learner SAY & DO is "EARS, EARS, EARS, EARS." After a while, music can be added, with children patting their head on the first part of the music and patting their ears on the second part. Additional ideas for working at this level of beat coordination can be found in *Movement Plus Music: Activities for Children Ages 3 to 7* (Weikart, 1989).

Level II: Single alternating movements

Children perform a single movement on one side of the body and then repeat the same movement with the corresponding body part on the other side of the body. This single alternating movement pattern continues. Example: While saying "KNEE, KNEE, KNEE, KNEE," children match with words the movement with one hand touching the knee, then the other hand touching the knee, and so on, in an alternating pattern.

Presenting a Level III Activity Using the Levels of Beat Coordination

1. Demonstrate the movements you want the children to try, say "Watch me and do what I'm doing," then pat your knees one time followed by patting your shoulders one time.

2. Suggest that the children try the two movements. *You should not join in,* because you do not want to establish the timing for the movement. Each child should try the sequence to his or her own timing. Keep this time short.

3. Ask the children to watch you again. Then pat your knees and then pat your shoulders several times before adding the SAY & DO terms of "KNEES, SHOULDERS." Encourage the children to try it with you.

4. Suggest to the children that they all try together by saying "Let's see if we can do it all together." Start the movements, then add the language (the SAY & DO) and have the children join in so that all are performing the movement with the SAY & DO method.

5. Play an instrumental music selection (without words), such as "Brian Boru's March" on *Rhythmically Moving 1* and repeat the movement to the beat of the music. If the children are having difficulty, have them try saying the words softly. *Reminder:* You don't have to add music. Instead you can suggest or have a child suggest another sequence and proceed through the sequence again, or you can go on to a different activity.

The learner SAY & DO is "CHIN, CHIN, CHIN, CHIN" for this Level I single movement.

Level II is more challenging than Level I because of the alternating pattern. Young children who are trying to move their hands according to the visual cue of the leader, rather than according to the *auditory cue* of the words they are saying (SAY & DO), may find that following the visual demonstration is confusing to them. It is important to avoid requiring specific right-handed or left-handed responding from young children.

Usually Level II is performed at a faster tempo than Level I. Using the faster tempo returns children more quickly to the preferred side of their body on every other movement. This means that if the song or rhyme is organized by its macrobeat into groups of 2 beats, a different side is used for each of those 2 microbeats.

There is one exception to using microbeat for Level II: If the particular single alternating movement that you are using for the rhyme, song, or recording is rocking the whole body to one side followed by rocking the whole body to the other side, this side-to-side shifting of the body will be performed to the *macrobeat*. Compared to some other movements, rocking takes more time to complete.

Level II movement with learner SAY & DO is usually mastered by at least kindergarten age. However, when music is incorporated, it is best to wait until first grade to expect children to alternate the hands successfully to music. Single movements matched to single words spoken in repetition create the learner SAY & DO. Initiate and support many opportunities for children to alternate the feet (to march) in microbeat to instrumental recordings, rhymes, and songs.

Level III(A): Sequenced movements—two movements

Children combine two single movements into a two-movement sequence. They move two corresponding body parts (or one body part) to one location and then move them to a different location. Example: Both hands touch the knees and then the head. The learner SAY & DO is "KNEES,

HEAD, KNEES, HEAD." Children approaching age 5 might try one hand touching the knee and then the head, with the same sequence repeated several times on the one side. Repeat this sequence with the other hand.

In the **movement core** this is nonlocomotor movement, two sides, sequenced. The tempo used for the movement sequence approximates a macrobeat tempo. Movement executed with both sides of the body is the easiest for children (and learners of any age) to sequence when working at this level of coordination. Through kindergarten age, children usually need to continue to use both sides, rather than one side, for the movement sequence. (After that, children should perform the sequenced movement first with one side of the body at least four times, then with the other side at least four times.) Also, Level III movements are more successful when performed at a relatively slow tempo.

Some children who seem to lack coordination or who are not attending to the task might perform the correct movements but do so out of timing or in reverse order (in the above example, they might struggle to match the timing of the leader and end up moving from head to knees as others move from knees to head). They may be watching the visual cue of the leader, but they are unable to respond in a coordinated manner. For these children, watching and labeling

The children in these two photos are patting their tummies and then their knees in the sequence they have constructed.

the movements before joining in is helpful. Unfortunately this may not help the youngest children. However, there is a **simplify** strategy using static movement that is effective for all learners, including the youngest:

For children who are having difficulty responding quickly enough to the sequence that they see the leader doing, use this **simplify** strategy. Begin by introducing children to the sequence as two static movements. That is, perform the first movement and hold it for accurate copying, and then perform the second movement and hold it. Repeat this process, adding the labels to the two static movements. Continue doing the sequence as two static movements, but gradually shorten the pause between the two parts of the sequence until you have arrived at the desired tempo.

When working with this level, it is better to use a sequence of movements that have some tactile endpoint rather than a movement out in the air, such as "BEND, STRAIGHTEN." As mentioned earlier, younger children usually find it easier to use the name of a body part as the word they match with movement. *Movement Plus Music: Activities for Children Ages 3 to 7* (Weikart, 1989) contains additional ideas for working with this level of beat coordination.

Level III(B): Sequenced movements—three movements

Children perform, in repetition, a sequence of three movements. The sequence is made up of one movement and then a different movement performed two times. Example: Touch both knees for the first movement. Touch the shoulders two times (for the second movement and also the third movement). The learner SAY & DO is "KNEES, SHOULDERS, SHOULDERS." (A similar example would be the same movement performed in repetition, with only one hand touching the knee and then touching the shoulder twice, "KNEE, SHOULDER, SHOULDER.")

Because this three-movement pattern is more difficult than Level III(A), we recommend not introducing it until at least first grade; nevertheless, this level is explained here for those adults who work with older children as well as preschoolers. Some children may tend to do the first movement of the sequence twice, rather than the second movement twice, because this may seem easier to them. However, using a sequence made up of a distinct first movement followed by two like movements puts the emphasis on the first movement, which is the intent. For children having the tendency to repeat the first movement twice, a **simplify** strategy using static movement will be useful:

Simplify by using static movements in first presenting the three-movement sequence. Begin by placing both hands on the knees and pausing for the first static movement, and then bring them to the ears and pause each time for each of the second and third static movements. So far, this is similar to what you did for static movement for the Level III(A) movement sequence, except that now you are holding your first movement and then holding each of the last two movements in the sequence. Now progress from the static movement to dynamic movement, doing the three-movement sequence in repetition, "KNEES, EARS, EARS, KNEES, EARS, EARS," and so on.

Level IV: Sequences of movements combined—four movements

Both sides of the body perform four movements—two sequences of two movements each. Example: Both hands touch the knees and then the head and then add on another two-movement sequence of shoulders, head. The learner SAY & DO is "KNEES, HEAD, SHOULDERS, HEAD." A variation would be to do the sequence on one side of the body at a time, repeating the sequence at least four times before repeating on the other side.

Notice the use of head in both two-movement sequences as the second of each sequence. This routine is easier for the child than attempting four different movements; "HEAD, SHOULDERS, KNEES, TOES."

This level of coordination unites two sequences of Level III(A) movements to form a four-movement sequence. Though following a four-movement sequence requires increased skill and concentration on the part of the children, using learner SAY & DO usually results in a high level of success. Also, it is helpful to use the **simplify** strategy by breaking the four-movement sequence into the two Level III(A) sequences and doing each of those several times before combining them into the four movements.

Children entering kindergarten should have the ability to match four words with four movements performed on two sides, provided that the movements are performed in a fairly slow tempo, using learner SAY & DO. Performing four-movement sequences to music is not recommended for young children because it is very difficult for 3–5-year-old children to attend to the sequence of four movements and also to attend to the beat of the music.

Suggested Activities—Levels of Beat Coordination

1. Using the rhyme "Peas Porridge Hot," ask the children to copy your motion of patting the steady beat. After the movement has been done several times, say the anchor word four times to bring the children to synchronization, and then begin the rhyme: **"Peas** porridge **hot. Peas** porridge **cold. Peas** porridge **in** the pot, **nine** days **old."** The words in bold designate the macrobeat that matches the patting.

2. Make up a chant like **"HEAD, SHOULDERS, KNEES, TOES."** Say this three times, and then say **"That's** the **way** the **move**ment **goes!"** or **"Now** it's **time** to **pat** our **nose."** Another example would be **HEAD, KNEES, CHIN, KNEES. Now** let's **all** pre**tend** to **sneeze!"** Be certain to move slowly and encourage the children to think of new rhyming words to vary the chant.

3. Ask a child to volunteer to show a motion. Help the child add a word to the motion he or she demonstrates to create a SAY & DO process. If the child's motion is too complex to add words to, help the child modify the

motion, so a SAY & DO can be created. Encourage all the children to try the motion first and then add the words. Have the child who volunteered the idea start the movement and add the chant.

Extending the Levels of Beat Coordination

Walking to the steady beat

Refer to the key experience *feeling and expressing steady beat* for information about walking to the beat. The strategies used in promoting that key experience should assist children who are not walking to the beat. Please remember that stepping or marching in personal space is easier for young children than marching or walking in general space.

When children have not had opportunities to march or step to the steady beat of a rhyme, song, or musical selection before the age of 3, it may be more difficult for them later on. To counteract this, caregivers, teachers, and parents can introduce toddlers to marching in parades and can continue supporting marching parades at the preschool level. Remember, though, that singing games and recordings with words sung or with action songs that put the beat in the feet, usually are not as appropriate for young children because the focus goes to the words and the fun of the activity, not to the steady beat. Try using instrumental music, without words, plus rhymes and songs to help children keep steady beat in the feet while listening. This strategy helps children develop the ability to alternate the feet in steady beat.

Clapping

The **levels of beat coordination** do not include clapping, since this is a difficult movement for children to do to the beat and also to sequence with other movements. When sequencing clapping with other movements, children must learn to change the plane of the movement as they bring their hands together.

There are two basic kinds of clapping. The first is primitive midline clapping, which the young child is capable of performing. In this type of clapping, both hands are doing the same thing with the same intensity in each hand. The second type of clapping, the type we ask older children and adults to do, requires one hand to become the target and the other hand to perform the beating motions. This latter type of clapping is not possible until the child is capable of inhibiting (holding still) the target hand while continuing the movement with the beater hand. Most children will use primitive midline clapping, if clapping is used. At this point, one might ask, "So what?" The rationale for avoiding clapping movements stems from a phenomenon in motor development known as "muscle memory." If one practices something in the same way over and over, it becomes "second nature." Thus, in the clapping situation, one soon will be less able to change to the more mature way of target-and-beater clapping. Also, the more primitive form of clapping is very difficult to use in identifying steady beat and in movement sequences. When rhymes, songs, and musical selections are involved, clapping can become so loud children no longer pay attention to the words or music.

As noted earlier, children in preschool find it easiest to perform movement in which both sides of the body are free to move as desired, rather than one side having to anchor (inhibit) while the other side moves. Holding an instrument in one hand while trying to play it with the other hand is another inhibited action that is difficult for many preschool children to do.

Introducing action songs, movement rhymes, singing games, and finger plays

Action songs, rhymes that have movement accompaniment, singing games, and finger plays are very difficult for young children to perform accurately and can be frustrating for them. Finger plays are the most difficult because they involve fine-motor movements. These are more appropriate for children of kindergarten age or older. When supporting young children who are engaged in movement rhymes, action songs, and singing games, several strategies can be useful:

1. Use only four movements with the rhyme or song. Taking the "Eensy Weensy Spider" as an example, remove "wash the spider out" and "dried up all the rain" and you will have a four-movement action song.

2. Do the movement sequences before adding the rhyme or song. This strategy does not mean that the entire rhyme or song has to be introduced with movement before melody and words are added. In fact, in some cases it is effective to do part of the movement and add that part of the rhyme or song.

3. Select rhymes and songs at first that only have two movements, like "Little Green Frog" from *Movement Plus Rhymes, Songs, & Singing Games* (Weikart, 1997).

4. At first, select activities in which children remain in their personal space.

5. Encourage children to explore movements in their own way. "Out came the sun" from "Eensy Weensy Spider" does not have to be performed in the same way by all the children. By using verbal directions (the **separate** strategy of the **teaching model**) you will encourage children to respond with their own ideas. Remember that rhymes and songs that use "right" and "left" need to be changed to "one side," to "other side," or to "two sides."

6. Pause after each phrase in the song or rhyme to give the children time to do the movement that phrase suggests. In "Eensy Weensy Spider," for example, pause after "went up the water spout" until all children have finished their movement; then go on and pause after "down came the rain and washed the spider out" leaving the movement out for the last part of the phrase, as suggested above.

Summary of Moving in Sequences to a Common Beat

Beat coordination, the observable outcome of this key experience, is achieved as children are exposed to and progress through the four **levels of beat coordination** for young children summarized in Chart 4.6 on page 148.

Ideally, young children will develop a basic understanding of these levels before they enter kindergarten. The most powerful movement learning strategy

we can give children is the ability to use learner SAY & DO. This cognitive-motor link permits increased concentration and unlocks children's potential to respond to movement that is visually demonstrated or presented with verbal directions.

The four **levels of beat coordination** provide a sequence of movement that progresses from simple to more complex motor tasks. **Beat coordination,** along with **basic timing** (steady beat independence), which was the outcome of the preceding key experience, is necessary for much knowledge construction in school and indeed throughout life. Any task children undertake that requires accurate timing appears to depend on their success in these two key experience areas.

Chart 4.6

Moving in Sequences to a Common Beat Result in Beat Coordination

Guidelines: Single or sequenced movements are repeated.
Link each movement to a single word (learner SAY & DO process).
Repeat each sequence a minimum of eight times. Incorporate music as appropriate.

Level		When Using Musical Selections
I	**Single Movement** Do the same *single* movement on both sides of the body for each beat.	(Macrobeat, nonlocomotor)
II	**Single Alternating Movements** Do the same *single* movement, with an alternate side of the body for each beat.	(Microbeat)
III(A)	**Sequenced Movements—two movements** Both sides sequence the same two movements.	(Macrobeat, nonlocomotor)
III(B)	**Sequenced Movements—three movements** Both sides sequence the same three movements (second and third movements are the same).	(Microbeat)
IV	**Sequenced Movements Combined—four movements** Two sides of the body sequence four movements (two Level III sequences combined).	(Macrobeat, nonlocomotor)

When children demonstrate comfort, awareness, and understanding, and have succeeded in each of the eight preschool **movement key experiences** areas, you can be sure that the foundation has been built—that the High/Scope *Education Through Movement—Building the Foundation* program has accomplished its goals. Your children

- Will truly be **engaged** in learning

- Will be **enabled** not only in movement but in all areas of learning

- Will have **extended** their movement skills toward movement and timing proficiency

Children will have learned to move so they can move to learn!

These boys are extending their movement skills toward movement and timing proficiency as one of them pats the tambourine to a steady beat and they all march to that beat.

Checklist for Adults 5

This book contains numerous suggestions for engaging and supporting young children successfully and appropriately in eight movement key experiences. This chapter summarizes these guidelines. Underlying all the suggestions is the general caution to keep the movement experiences simple to assure children's success. Another general rule of thumb is to work with children *at their level* and exhibit a supportive and encouraging manner.

Young children are great at picking up on our slightest cues—both positive and negative! They want to succeed at whatever they attempt. Movement experiences can serve to strengthen a child's emerging self-confidence and independence, but for this to happen we must protect the child's fragile ego and support his or her interests and choices. The best way to do this is to provide a comfortable and supportive environment, and to encourage children to take the initiative and be leaders.

Following is a checklist that covers the general guidelines for introducing movement experiences to children as well as specific guidelines for each of the eight movement key experiences.

General Guidelines for Movement Experiences

 Are you helping children build on their existing motor skills rather than "teaching" them a whole new set of skills? Your role is one of guidance and support. Sometimes we initiate movement activities that are too difficult for young children. Children need movement opportunities that are based on naturally occurring activities and situations, so that they can experience basic movements in a safe, familiar, and secure environment. Children need lots of practice time, too, and they need to practice in their own way.

 Are you frequently joining in the children's play activities? Children respond best to adults who join in and play with them— adults who meet the children at their level. Doing the movements with the children will increase their self-confidence and make them more willing to try to do what you are doing.

 Are you designing movement tasks to assure children's success? Try to avoid situations in which you are put in the position of correcting the child who is "not doing it right." The movement experience should have no "rights" and "wrongs."

 Are you encouraging the children to lead various activities? Once children are comfortable with a movement activity, suggest that they lead it in their own way. Depending on the activity and the length of time available, one, a few, or all of the children can be leaders. Over time, make sure that every child has a chance to lead some activities.

Are you waiting for the children to volunteer and make their own choices and decisions? If children who haven't volunteered are called on to choose a new way to do a movement, they may not be ready to do so. In time, once these children see the comfort that other children have in suggesting new kinds of movement or movement variations, they will be eager to volunteer. Be patient. It may take considerable time for some children to have enough confidence to volunteer.

 Are you initiating movement activities at appropriate times during the daily routine? Excellent times in the day to initiate movement activities are at the beginning or end of the day, during transition times, at the start of large-group or small-group times, at outside time. Adults can set aside a block of time for movement activities at least three times per week if movement time every day is not possible.

 Are you providing adequate space for activities that develop children's gross-motor abilities? Arrange your classroom to provide adequate space for large-group, small-group, and individual movement activities. Keep in mind that many movement activities can be done during outdoor time, too.

Key Experience: Acting Upon Movement Directions

 Are you using only one of the three presentation methods at a time? Give verbal directions *or* silently demonstrate the movement *or* silently provide tactile guidance. Children respond better when you use only one presentation method.

 Are you keeping the movement simple for young children? Movements that involve moving one area of the body at a time are easier for young children to perform than movements that involve moving all areas of the body. For example, move just the arms or just the legs. Movements in the upper body are easier for children to perform than movements in the lower body. For example, bending and straightening the arms is easier than bending and straightening the legs. Also, moving on one's own is easier than moving with a partner or engaging in synchronized group movements.

 Are you frequently introducing movements for both sides of the body? When a person makes symmetrical movements, he or she moves both sides of the body in the same way at the same time; for example, the person moves both arms or both legs together while seated. It is important that children perform such movements to exercise their nonpreferred side as well as their preferred side.

 When children move one side of the body, are you suggesting that they repeat the movement on the other side? Most children will choose to move first on their preferred side, so encourage them to repeat the movement on the nonpreferred side as well. In the long run, this will help the children develop more complex motor skills.

 Are you making sure that the children can easily see your demonstration or hear your suggestions for movements? Do all the children have an unobstructed view of you? It is easy to forget that children sitting alongside you will not be able to see well; suggest that they move to a better vantage point.

 Are you avoiding specifying "right" and "left" when referring to sides of the body? Young children need to respond to movement directions without having to think about which side of the body to use. Wait until children are in second grade to ask them to do this. This does not mean that we never mention right or left, only that we do not ask the children to identify or specify sides in this manner.

Key Experience: Describing Movement

 Are you asking the children questions that make them think about a movement and the various steps involved in it? Encourage children to describe what they are doing while they are doing it. In the case of a faulty movement pattern, first have the children do that movement and describe it before suggesting a change in the faulty pattern. When offering such a suggestion, do so in a complimentary way: "Yes, Johnny, I can see that you were turning your arm all the way around. Can you just swing it back and forth like this?" (You then demonstrate.)

Are you asking children to plan what they are going to do before they do it? Encourage children to think ahead and to conceptualize their movements before they actually do them. You may wish to record their plan for them or ask them to draw a picture of what they plan to do.

 Are you having children recall a movement they have just completed? Encourage children to describe a movement they have completed and to compare what they did to what they planned to do. This review process will help children follow through on their plans and activities.

Are you showing children how to use the SAY & DO method? It helps children to be able to link a movement to a word that labels or describes the movement. In this case the word (SAY) and movement (DO) occur simultaneously.

Key Experience: Moving in Nonlocomotor Ways

 Are you helping children move comfortably? Give children lots of opportunities to move comfortably from various nonlocomotor positions. Encourage children to explore these movements in their own way.

 Are you helping children understand and describe the types of movements that they can do while standing, sitting, or lying in one spot? Children need opportunities to develop this type of *body awareness* by engaging in various types of nonlocomotor movements. You can promote *language awareness* as well by suggesting that the children label and talk about their nonlocomotor movements. Children can also develop *space* and *time* awareness if you ask questions that give them opportunities to think about where and how they moved or will move.

Key Experience: Moving in Locomotor Ways

 Are you helping children develop the confidence to move about freely and comfortably in the room or area? Give children lots of opportunities to move about the room or outdoor area. They should develop the ability to avoid bumping into others as they move about. Also, to increase their ability to control their bodies, encourage them to practice ending their movements without falling down.

 Are you helping children understand fully the types of movements they can do as they move about freely? Give children plenty of opportunities to explore the five basic movements involving weight transfer that are described in Chapter 3 and to learn the labels that are used for these locomotor movements.

 Are you helping children develop and strengthen their awareness of space and time through locomotor movements? As children learn to vary their locomotor movements, you can help them develop a fuller awareness of space and time by asking questions that define the "where" and "how" of the movement pattern.

Key Experience: Moving With Objects

 Are you encouraging children to practice the motor pattern first—before they actually move with objects? I have found that children who have difficulty throwing, kicking, or striking a ball; printing and writing; or playing a musical instrument often have not had many opportunities to practice the motor patterns required *before* using the objects. Show them how to do this, and they will use this technique again and again as they master various movement patterns.

 When introducing the use of balls, are you giving children enough time to develop skill in manipulating a ball on their own before suggesting group activities? Provide each child with opportunities to explore alone with a ball before suggesting partners for tossing or kicking a ball and before introducing games involving balls.

Key Experience: Expressing Creativity in Movement

 Are you giving children opportunities to create their own movements? When introducing this key experience, it is helpful to offer movement problems for children to solve. Remember to provide enough structure at first (problem solving) and then remove some of that structure as the children become comfortable with this key experience.

Are you encouraging children to use representation in their movements? Suggest that the children move "as if" they were familiar objects or were involved in familiar situations.

Key Experience: Feeling and Expressing Beat

 Are you asking young children to move to the steady beat of rhymes, songs, and instrumental music? Give children plenty of opportunities to move to the steady beat. Do not confuse this with moving to the *rhythm* of word patterns, or to the *syllables* of words. Third grade is a more appropriate time to introduce children to movement that uses rhythm, and then to different note values, not syllables of words.

 Are you playing instrumental music as children practice moving to an external beat? Music with lyrics may draw the child's attention away from the task at hand. To avoid this, use instrumental music when you want children to move to an external beat.

 Are you using movements against the body? Movements with tactile endpoints are easier than movements performed in the air. Also, rocking in groups is another easy and enjoyable motion to use in feeling and expressing steady beat, as is touching both hands to the floor.

Key Experience:
Moving in Sequences to a Common Beat

 Are you helping children develop the body coordination they need to be successful with group movements? Build the child's body coordination by using the four **levels of beat coordination** described in Chapter 4. Avoid inhibited movements (for example, one kind of clapping) in which the child must anchor one side of the body while moving the other side. These types of movements are best introduced to children in second grade.

 When you suggest that children move in sequences to a common beat, are you starting off with movements in which children touch body parts or the floor? It is easier for children to have a tactile point of contact as they express the common beat. It's more difficult for them to follow the steady beat if they must move their arms or legs about in space, with no point of contact for the movement.

 Are you providing children with enough practice time before having them move in sequence to a common beat? Children need time to try out a particular group movement on their own, before they perform the movement with others to a common beat. Encourage them to use the SAY & DO method as they practice by themselves.

 Are you helping the children learn the movements first for rhymes, action songs, chants, and singing games? Children should be very familiar with the movements involved in a rhyme, action song, or singing game before they try singing and moving at the same time. The language may distract them when they are trying to learn the movements. It is therefore advisable to present the movements first and then add the words when the children are comfortable with and fully aware of the movements.

Finally, do you know the "golden rules"? As you introduce the key experiences in movement to young children, keep these final "golden rules" in mind:

1. **Keep them short.**
2. **Keep them simple**
3. **Make them enjoyable.**
4. **Design them to assure success.**
5. **Suggest rather than *direct.***

References

Carlton, E. B., & Weikart, P. S. 1994. *Foundations in Elementary Education: Music*. Ypsilanti, MI: High/Scope Press.

Carlton, E. B., & Weikart, P. S. 1996–1999. *Guides to Rhythmically Moving 1–4*.

Gordon, E. 1984. *Learning Sequences in Music* (Chapter 4). Chicago: GIA Publishing.

Hannaford, C. 1998, November. "Movement and the Brain." *Teaching Elementary Physical Education* 9(6), 18.

Hannaford, C. 1995. *Smart Moves: Why Learning Is Not All in Your Head*. Arlington, VA: Great Ocean Publishers.

Healy, J. 1990. *Endangered Minds, Why Children Don't Think and What We Can Do About It*. NY: Simon & Schuster.

Hohmann, M., & Weikart, D. P. 1995. *Educating Young Children: Active Learning Practices for Preschool and Child Care Programs*. Ypsilanti, MI: High/Scope Press.

Jensen, E. 1998. *Teaching With the Brain in Mind*. Alexandria, VA: Association for Supervision and Curriculum Development.

Kessler, R. G. 1994, October. "Idealogical and Civil Liberties: Implications of the Public Health Approach to Guns, Crime, and Violence." *Journal of Pediatrics*.

Longden, S. H., & Weikart, P. S. 1998. *Cultures and Styling in Folk Dance*. Ypsilanti, MI: High/Scope Press.

Pica, R. 1996, December. "Early Childhood Physical Education." *Teaching Elementary Physical Education* 7(6), 6.

Tomlinson-Keasey, C. 1985. *Child Development: Psychological, Sociocultural, and Biological Factors*. Homewood, IL: Dorsey Press.

Weikart, P. S. 1990. *Movement in Steady Beat*. Ypsilanti, MI: High/Scope Press.

Weikart, P. S. 1989. *Movement Plus Music: Activities for Children Ages 3 to 7,* 2nd ed. Ypsilanti, MI: High/Scope Press.

Weikart, P. S. 1997. *Movement Plus Rhymes, Songs, & Singing Games,* 2nd ed. Ypsilanti, MI: High/Scope Press.

Weikart, P. S., creative director. 1983–1985. *Rhythmically Moving 1–9* (music recordings). Ypsilanti, MI: High/Scope Press.

Weikart, P. S. 1997. *Teaching Folk Dance: Successful Steps*. Ypsilanti, MI: High/Scope Press.

Weikart, P. S. 1998. *Teaching Movement & Dance: A Sequential Approach to Rhythmic Movement,* 4th ed. Ypsilanti, MI: High/Scope Press.

Weikart, P. S. & Carlton, E. B. 1995. *Foundations in Elementary Education: Movement*. Ypsilanti, MI: High/Scope Press.

Index

About the Author

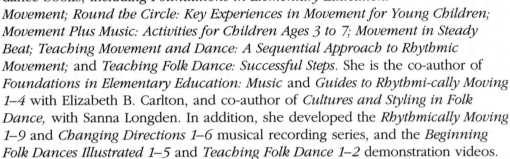

Phyllis S. Weikart, Director of the High/Scope *Education Through Movement: Building the Foundation* program, is one of the country's leading authorities on movement-based active learning. She bases her approach to teaching on her ongoing work with students of all ages—from preschoolers to senior citizens. She is the author of numerous movement and dance books, including *Foundations in Elementary Education: Movement; Round the Circle: Key Experiences in Movement for Young Children; Movement Plus Music: Activities for Children Ages 3 to 7; Movement in Steady Beat; Teaching Movement and Dance: A Sequential Approach to Rhythmic Movement;* and *Teaching Folk Dance: Successful Steps.* She is the co-author of *Foundations in Elementary Education: Music* and *Guides to Rhythmi-cally Moving 1–4* with Elizabeth B. Carlton, and co-author of *Cultures and Styling in Folk Dance,* with Sanna Longden. In addition, she developed the *Rhythmically Moving 1–9* and *Changing Directions 1–6* musical recording series, and the *Beginning Folk Dances Illustrated 1–5* and *Teaching Folk Dance 1–2* demonstration videos.

Associate Professor Emeritus in the Division of Kinesiology, University of Michigan, and visiting Associate Professor at Hartt School of Music, Weikart is also Movement Consultant for the High/Scope Educational Research Foundation. Her formal education includes a B.S. degree from Beaver College in Pennsylvania and an M.A. degree from the University of Michigan. In addition to being a nationally known and highly respected educator-author, Weikart is a researcher, curriculum developer, workshop leader, choreographer, and promoter of high-quality international folk dance recordings. Through her wide-ranging experiences, Phyllis S. Weikart has developed an approach to teaching that ensures the success of both teachers and students.

Movement-Related Resources From High/Scope®

Movement in Steady Beat

This manual presents a collection of unique rhymes and action songs for children aged 3 to 7. Focuses on the movement key experience *feeling and expressing beat*.

BK-M1007 $14.95

P. S. Weikart. Soft cover, 96 pages, 1990. 0-929816-08-0.

Movement Plus Music: Activities for Children Ages 3 to 7, 2nd ed.

Outlines movement activities for young children and gives suggestions for synchronizing the activities to music. Focuses on moving in coordinated ways, following directions, feeling and expressing the beat, and moving creatively. This edition updates many movement activities and suggests more music from the *Rhythmically Moving* 1–4 CDs and cassettes and *Round the Circle* book.

BK-M1005 $10.95

P. S. Weikart. Soft cover, 40 pages, 1989. 0-931114-96-9.

Movement Plus Rhymes, Songs, & Singing Games, 2nd ed.

A revised collection of engaging movement activities for children. The activities supplement those described in *Round the Circle* and provide age-appropriate movement experiences. Use them during large-group time, small-group time, or transitions.

BK-M1013 $14.95

P. S. Weikart et al. Soft cover, 100 pages, 1997. 1-57379-066-4.

Movement Plus Rhymes, Songs, & Singing Games—Recordings

Colorful, appropriate music to accompany the enjoyable activities for children found in the companion book.

Cassette: BK-M2010-C $10.95; CD: BK-M2210 $15.95

P. S. Weikart, creative director, 1997.
Cassette 1-57379-067-2 or CD 1-57379-030-3.

Rhythmically Moving 1–9

Music for parents and teachers of all ages. Includes suggestions for use with *Teaching Folk Dance: Successful Steps and Teaching Movement & Dance: A Sequential Approach to Rhythmic Movement*. Can also be used with the *Beginning Folk Dances Illustrated* video series. Select one or all of these recordings—there is no special order or level of difficulty.

P. S. Weikart, creative director. Cassettes or CDs.

Rhythmically Moving 1:

All the Way to Galway, Sliding, Happy Feet, Oh, How Lovely, Gaelic Waltz, Southwind, Arkansas Traveler/Sailors Hornpipe/ Turkey in the Straw, and more!

Cassette: BK-M2001-C $10.95; CD: BK-M2201 $15.95

Cassette 0-931114-64-0 or CD 0-929816-13-7.

Rhythmically Moving 2:

Rakes of Mallow, Seven Jumps, Djurdjevka Kolo, Limbo Rock, Blackberry Quadrille, Fjaskern, Yankee Doodle, and more!

Cassette: BK-M2002-C $10.95; CD: BK-M2202 $15.95

Cassette 0-931114-65-9 or CD 0-929816-14-5.

Rhythmically Moving 3:

Irish Washerwoman, Alley Cat, Cumberland Square, Bele Kawe, Mexican Mixer, Hora Medura, Erev Shel Shoshanim, and more!

Cassette: BK-M2003-C $10.95; CD: BK-M2203 $15.95

Cassette 0-931114-66-7 or CD 0-929816-15-3.

Rhythmically Moving 4:

Spanish Coffee, Apat-Apat, Sneaky Snake, Ersko Kolo, Zemer Atik, Bekendorfer Quadrille, Hava Nagila, Hineh Ma Tov, and more!

Cassette: BK-M2004-C $10.95; CD: BK-M2204 $15.95

Cassette 0-931114-67-5 or CD 0-929816-16-1.

Rhythmically Moving 5:

Jamaican Holiday, Twelfth Street Rag, Corrido, Entertainer, Carnavalito, Ajde Noga Za Nogama, Hora Hassidit, and more!

Cassette: BK-M2005-C $10.95; CD: BK-M2205 $15.95

Cassette 0-931114-68-3 or CD 0-929816-29-3.

Rhythmically Moving 6:

Good Old Days, Sicilian Tarantella, Iste Hendek, Pata Pata, Tipsy, Dimna Juda, Savila Se Bela Loza, Niguno Shel Yossi, and more!

Cassette: BK-M2006-C $10.95; CD: BK-M2206 $15.95

Cassette 0-931114-69-1 or CD 0-929816-30-7.

Rhythmically Moving 7:

Bossa Nova, Sellenger's Round, Ais Girgis, Jambo, Popcorn, D'Hammerschmiedsgselln, Sweet Girl, Tant Hessie, and more!

Cassette: BK-M2007-C $10.95; CD: BK-M2207 $15.95

Cassette 0-931114-70-5 or CD 0-929816-31-5.

Rhythmically Moving 8:

Jessie Polka, Misirlou, Hora Agadati, Bulgarian Dance #1, Amos Moses, Korobushka, Hot Pretzels, Leor Chiyuchech, and more!

Cassette: BK-M2008-C $10.95; CD: BK-M2208 $15.95

Cassette 0-931114-71-3 or CD 0-929816-32-3.

Rhythmically Moving 9:

Salty Dog Rag, Instant Success, Chiotikos, The Hustle, Armenian Misirlou, Hora Bialik, Debka Daluna, Tanko Bushi, and more!

Cassette: BK-M2009-C $10.95; CD: BK-M2209 $15.95

Cassette 0-931114-72-1 or CD 0-929816-33-1.

To order these or any other High/Scope® products, contact High/Scope® Press: phone (800)40-PRESS fax (800)442-4FAX
To see a full listing of High/Scope® preschool products, visit our Web site: www.highscope.org